EARTHQUAKES AND VOLCANOES

EARTHQUAKES AND VOLCANOES

Dr Robert Muir Wood

Weidenfeld & Nicolson
New York

CONTENTS

Editor James Hughes
Art Editor Paul Drayson
Picture Research Millicent Trowbridge
Assistant Editor Julia Gorton
Production Androulla Pavlou

Maps and diagrams by Mulkern
Rutherford

Edited and designed by
Mitchell Beazley International Ltd,
Artists House, 14–15 Manette St,
London W1V 5LB

VOLCANOES AND
EARTHQUAKES
A Mitchell Beazley Earth Science
Handbook

Published by Weidenfeld & Nicolson,
New York
A Division of Wheatland Corporation
10 East 53rd Street
New York, NY 10022

Library of Congress
Cataloging-in-Publication Data
Wood, Robert Muir
Earthquakes and volcanoes
(A Mitchell Beazley earth science
handbook)
Includes index.
1. Earthquakes – Popular works. 2.
Volcanoes –
Popular works. I. Title. II. Series
QE521.2.W66 1987 551.2'2 86-24691
ISBN 1-55584-083-3

Filmsetting by
Hourds Typographica, Stafford,
England
Origination by
Gilchrist Bros. Ltd, Leeds, England
Printed and bound by
Printer Portuguesa LDA, Portugal

First American Edition 1987
10 9 8 7 6 5 4 3 2 1

When time stood still

Countdown to catastrophe

It was early morning in Mexico City, a few minutes after 7.00. The sun was just rising over the mountain bowl. The distant volcanoes to the south were obscured only by the familiar Mexico City smog. In countless homes – from the grand ranches of the suburbs to the crowded apartment buildings and fringing shanty towns – many of the 18 million inhabitants of the most densely populated city on Earth were waking and getting ready to go to work, or to school; washing, dressing and breakfasting. Some early risers were traveling, others were already in their offices. In those places in any great city where work must go on around the clock, there were telephone operators, porters, and policemen on duty, while in the hospitals the night staff were making way for new teams of nurses and doctors to begin the daily round in the crowded wards. In the streets, the morning rush-hour chaos was beginning.

It was breakfast time, a few minutes before 8.00, on the morning of May 8. Another sweltering day seemed imminent in the cobbled streets of the town of St. Pierre, on the island of Martinique in the Caribbean. The townspeople had various preoccupations – the volcano of Mt Pelée, located a few miles to the north, was making life difficult for them with its continued noisy eruption, leaving dirty ash over the streets and houses. The main headline in the

Downtown Mexico City along the Paseo de la Reforma, shortly before the devastating earthquake of 1985. Despite its appearance to the contrary, this impressive array of metal, glass and concrete buildings – symbols of wealth and permanence – is fundamentally vulnerable in the face of natural forces (*see* page 10).

daily paper, however, concerned the forthcoming elections. Three days earlier, a plague of venomous snakes had emerged from the surrounding jungle to take refuge in the town, and a boiling mudslide had poured down a side valley of the volcano, overwhelming a sugar mill. Yet what was there to fear? The island's governor had returned to town to show the people that their volcano was no more than a noisy and dirty inconvenience.

It was 9.40am on All Saints Day, a fine Saturday morning, and many of the people of Lisbon were attending church to pray for their ancestors. Lisbon, capital of Portugal and center of a great empire in the Americas, was an elegant and wealthy port. After more than two centuries of exploration, of plunder and trade in gold, silver and spices, the wealth was conspicuous in the buildings and churches. Many merchants had houses filled with rich tapestries and furnishings, and paintings by the great European masters were to be found in the city's palaces. A fine new quay had recently been completed in marble on the banks of the River Tagus to receive ships returning from the colonies in the Far East and in the Americas.

It was mid-afternoon: a few minutes before 3.00 on May 22. The southern winter was just beginning in the city of Valdivia, Chile.

The river wound slowly through the tree-lined streets of this old Spanish colonial town, with its estuarine harbor – a perfect refuge on an exposed and stormy coast. The large number of German immigrants, together with the temperate climate, gave the town a mid-European feel. This was enhanced by the appearance of the buildings, many of which had imitated Central European town styles with false stucco exteriors of metal and plaster, laid onto the wooden and stone frames.

It was just after 5.30pm on the afternoon of March 27, a cold Good Friday at the end of a long Alaskan winter. Anchorage was a pioneer town, a town that had grown like the plants that gradually colonize wasteland – first a few shacks, then some more established houses, and then tall concrete offices and stores, with new fringing developments of wealthy suburbs. The temperature was still a few degrees below freezing and most of the people were at home on this holiday, preparing their meals, or watching television. With light snow and rain falling, there was little reason to be outside in the early evening gloom.

It was 7.30pm, just after dark in the mountain villages of Basilicata, southern Italy. These towns had changed little in a hundred years – a few new apartment buildings and schools had been built on their outskirts, but as they crowned the mountain tops, there was little space in which to expand. Some small stores were still open on this cold November evening, and there was a bustle of activity through the narrow streets and up the steep paths that ran between the high houses. In many homes, dinner was being served, and in the small bars, farmers were drinking wine and talking.

It was 11.00pm in Armero, Colombia, a large sprawling town of white colonial, wooden, concrete and sheet metal shacks, set in a wide plain at the foot of the mountains where the Lagunillas River emerged from a narrow ravine. The relative prosperity of the town was dependent on rich crops of coffee, rice, fruit and cotton, grown with the help of fertile volcanic soils and the frequent heavy rains. Since 5.30pm that evening a soft fall of volcanic ash had been settling on the town, like some exotic tropical snow, and an hour later, a storm of rain had thrown up a smell of sulfur. The townspeople knew that the much discussed eruption of the volcano of Nevado del Ruiz, nearly 5,500m (18,000ft) high and 40km (25 miles) to the west of them, had finally begun. As the ash began to fall, some had thought to leave their town, but a public announcement at the church had reinforced the message from the local radio station that advised calm. Now, after an evening of argument and concern about the eruption, the 23,000 inhabitants of Armero had mostly gone to bed. The power supply had failed several times, but the local radio station continued to play soothing night music.

It was beginning to get light, soon after 3.30am on the summer night of July 28. The dull gray sky in the hour before dawn matched the sprawling industrial landscape of the city of Tangshan.

In its heyday: St. Pierre on the Caribbean island of Martinique, known in the 1890s as the "Paris of the Caribbean". Built on the profits of cane sugar grown on the rich volcanic soil, it was a wealthy port until that fateful day in May 1902 (*see* page 12).

The first light illuminated the crude apartment blocks, and factories of concrete and brick peppered with a forest of thousands of factory chimneys. A million people lived and worked in this great coal mining and industrial center of northern China. While the majority slept, many of the heavy engineering plants continued to work, sending up smoke plumes to join the perpetual city smog. Trains edged slowly through the great railway junctions, and 30,000 miners toiled underground, working the thick coal seams that lay beneath the city.

Let us stop the clock, freeze the frame of the lives of these towns at these times. In Mexico City it was a time as ordinary, as everyday, as the instant in which you are reading these words. In Tangshan the night was no more than an ordinary night and the people slept soundly in their beds. In Valdivia the day was no different from other days, there was cooking and talking and working and shopping. In St. Pierre and Armero, a nearby volcano had begun to erupt like many neighboring volcanoes had before, and apart from the inconvenience, what reason was there for alarm? Eruptions come and go like the sugar cane or the coffee harvest.

At all these places there was no sense of foreboding, no imminent sense of doom. The possibility that their houses might suddenly be thrown to the ground seemed to the people of Basilicata as incredible as it would be for you, as you read this, should the room or building suddenly collapse around you. If you had mentioned to the wealthy inhabitants of the Turnagain Heights suburb of Anchorage that the earth beneath them was about to give way, they would have laughed.

Yet in all these towns, at all these unremarkable moments, time became frozen, the clock was about to stop. The most ordinary routines of people's lives were about to become transformed.

Disaster strikes

At 7.18am, the Earth broke beneath the Pacific Coast of Mexico, but it was not until a whole minute later that the shock of this fracture reached Mexico City 400km (250 miles) away. On the outskirts of the city people noticed the shaking, but it did little damage, and after clearing up a few small broken objects the people went on with their day, irritated by power cuts, and the loss of telephone connections but unalarmed by the event. Yet in the very heart of the city, what was no more than a prolonged tremor in the outskirts had become an ominous rhythmic storm of massive vibrations.

As the slow shaking grew more powerful, the huge public building of Nuevo León – 14 stories high, 180m (600ft) long and home to 400 families – began to give way. Starting at the north end, the whole structure crumpled in on itself, floor by floor, crushing the intervening partition walls, furniture and occupants. The middle portion of the building then toppled outward, smashing as it fell, and breaking off at the third floor like a tree blown down by the wind. The old Regis Hotel in the city center also crashed down upon itself. At the National Medical Center hospital, the building

The collapsed Tlaltelolco Apartment Complex, Mexico City, after the earthquake of September 19 1985. The furiously vibrating building simply tore itself apart. Reinforced concrete warped and ripped like plastic. The rescuers had to mine through a tangle of steel reinforcing bars and concrete slabs in the search for survivors.

warped and folded, while a doctors' living quarters collapsed, and the maternity center was completely crushed. At the Benito Juarez hospital, 1,000 workers and patients, including the overlapping shifts of doctors and nurses, were all buried beneath the falling central tower. Several dozen schools collapsed, though before any pupils had arrived.

It would take many days of grim digging into the ruins to find that altogether around 10,000 people had been killed, almost half of that number in only four or five apartment buildings and hospitals. Yet of Mexico City's million or so buildings, only a tiny fraction of them, about 7,000, had suffered damage. A high proportion of these were between 7 and 15 stories tall, clustered in the city center.

There would be much to discover about this remarkable earthquake which inflicted terrible damage on buildings in a small area 400km (250 miles) away from its source, yet left villages and towns much closer to the epicenter unscathed. The year was 1985.

"A torrent of black fog"

At 7.50am, the volcanic mountain of Mt Pelée, north of St. Pierre, erupted. In a series of great explosions, red-hot gas and volcanic debris shot out of the mountain. Some of it went straight up in a billowing black cloud. Some of it was blasted out sideways, perhaps from the collapse of material from one of the explosions. Clinging to the mountain side, and guided by a notch in the crater wall, the deadly cloud raced down upon St. Pierre at about 200kph (120mph), reaching the town within 2 minutes.

One man who had a premonition that something was about to happen was a wealthy planter, Fernand Clerc, who had observed crazy fluctuations of his barometer at 7am. He bundled his wife and children into a carriage to make their escape, though he was unable to persuade any of his friends to accompany him. Three miles out of town in the hills, they turned to witness the momentous eruption, and watched with awe as the laterally-moving cloud toppled over, swooping down the hill, followed by a sheet of flame, "a great torrent of black fog," raging and thundering with a hellish roar. Soon Clerc and his family were plunged into a darkness so thick that they could no longer see each other. After 20 minutes of this hot suffocating ash fall, a powerful wind came to clear the air, and Clerc descended into St. Pierre. He found a holocaust. The town was totally devastated by the burning cloud, buildings everywhere were destroyed, timbers ablaze, and his relatives and friends all dead.

A ship of the Quebec Line, the *Roraima*, had been moored in the bay about half a mile from the land. As the fiery wind hit the ship, it sliced through the masts, smoke-stack, and rigging, and sent the vessel keeling over with its rail under the water. As different parts of the ship began to burn, a gluey ash was laid down on the skins of all those who had been sheltered from the initial blast. Only about 20 of the 68 passengers and crew survived. On land the situation was far worse. Throughout the city only two men survived the inferno: a young shoemaker who showed remarkable powers of resilience to the burning gases; and a prisoner, Auguste Ciparis, who owed his survival to his place of confinement – a little windowless dungeon in St. Pierre prison. The year was 1902.

Earthquake, wave, and fire

It was 9.40am when the huge structure of the Santa Maria cathedral in Lisbon gave a terrible shudder, causing the chandeliers to rattle and gyrate furiously. There was mass panic – the congregation rushed for the doors and took refuge in a small square outside the building, where they were joined by people pouring out of neighboring houses and churches.

As they all stood and prayed, a second, more violent quake hit the city, and the heavy stone façades of nearby buildings fell outward into the square, crushing all those who had fled outside to escape. The wealth of the city had been invested in stone – and now it was this same stone that was raining down on the citizens in the narrow medieval streets and in the houses. The church spires were "waving like a cornfield in the breeze" before they fell.

To escape from the buildings, many people had fled down to the new marble quay along the River Tagus out of the reach of falling masonry. Here, about 40 minutes after the first shock and at the

In a few minutes
(above) on the morning of
May 8 1902, St. Pierre on
Martinique was annihilated,
as if hit by an atom bomb.
A red-hot hurricane of gas
and ash had swooped down
from Mt Pelée to destroy
the town. Of 30,000
inhabitants there were only
two survivors.

**The destruction of
Lisbon** (left) on November
1 1755: but there were no
photographs to record it.
The events of many hours
have been telescoped into
this single print — falling
buildings, rushing tsunami
and the ensuing fire, which
together claimed more than
60,000 lives.

The wooden houses of Valdivia in southern Chile, wrecked as if battered by the sea. Waves in the ground from the largest earthquake of the century on May 22 1960 broke up the foundations. But the ground had also sunk: the whole city had subsided by almost 2m (7ft) and low-lying areas had been permanently flooded.

time of the second, the sea suddenly retreated. It then burst back with a mighty wave over 10m (33ft) high, which smashed the quay structure and overwhelmed all those who had sought refuge there. The wave returned twice more to smash ships, docks and the shoreline warehouses. Throughout the city, tumbled candles and kitchen fires had set alight the furnishings and timbers of numerous buildings, and soon these small fires had joined forces to form a wall of fire. This was swept by a northeast wind through much of the city, taking three days to consume everything in its path – houses, palaces, churches and warehouses.

One quarter of the city's population – more than 60,000 people – were crushed, drowned or burned alive and one of Europe's most prosperous cities had, in a matter of hours, been reduced to rubble and ashes, as if hit by an atom bomb. The year was 1755.

Sinking into the ground

At about 3.05pm, a strong shock was felt through Valdivia and also across the whole of southern Chile. Most of the people had left their houses and were talking in the streets when, ten minutes later, the earth began to roll silently and vibrate. The tops of the trees flailed, and chimneys crashed down. Many of the wooden houses were ripped from their foundations; others twisted and sank into the ground, which had liquefied beneath them. The pavements were slowly submerged by great boiling outbursts of sand. The rolling lasted a full three and half minutes.

Even when the shaking stopped, the effects of this enormous earthquake were not over. Out in the main estuary at the mouth of the river in the Bay of Corral, three Chilean merchant ships were moored. Ten minutes after the shaking had ceased, the water began to fall and then to rise again between 3-5m (10-16ft) above its normal level, flooding all the houses and factories at the port of Corral. At 3.30pm, the water began to rush out of the bay, drawing two of the merchant ships irresistibly with it. Half an hour later, an enormous mass of water burst into the bay in a gigantic wave 10m (33ft) high that smashed all the low-lying buildings. The water began to pour away at speeds of more than 30kph (20mph) dragging with it all the debris from the wooden houses and factories. A great trough of raging water 6-8m (20-25ft) wide and 10m (33ft) deep developed in the center of the bay, and a tugboat attempting to escape fell in a double somersault into the abyss, never to reemerge. After 20 minutes the bay was almost completely dry, and there were great waterfalls pouring in from the side rivers, scouring out millions of tons of sand and silt. A third wave came like the second, drawing with it some of the wooden houses earlier pulled out to sea, which were now piled in grotesque stacks along the waterline. A tugboat was thrown over the blast furnaces at Corral. Two of the three merchant ships were sunk as they were torn by the currents. The waves continued for more than a day.

In Valdivia itself, after the water waves had finally subsided, many of the streets and houses along the river remained submerged. The town and the countryside to both north and south had sunk by almost 2m (7ft). The earthquake caused damage along 1,000km (600 miles) of the coast of Chile. The death toll in Valdivia as across the whole region was remarkably low – only 150 died in the city and only 5,000 in the whole of Chile (the majority drowned by the great waves that followed the shaking). But for the ten-minute warning, the fatalities would have been far higher, for over 400,000 houses were destroyed. The year was 1960.

A scene of total destruction

At 5.36pm, the ground beneath Anchorage began to roll, first gently and then more violently as the shock waves tugged at the city. The ground itself began to break up, and along the main business street one whole side dropped 4m (13ft). In a house in the smartest of Anchorage's residential districts, Turnagain Heights, the publisher of the city's main daily newspaper had been sitting relaxing in his home, when the earth-waves began rolling in. He rushed outside and turned to see his fine house, writhing and twisting, the opposite ends pulling and compressing again. There was a terrible noise of breaking glass and wood, and the earth underneath the house began to open in great fissures. Suddenly the ground beneath his feet had vanished and he was plunged down the slopes of dry sand into a channel, which continued to widen, filling up all the while with trees, timber posts, and frozen soil. By the time he had climbed out of the ravine the noise had ceased, but the scene was one of total destruction. A mile and a half of headland

The wealthy suburb (right) of Turnagain
Heights outside Anchorage, Alaska in the
aftermath of the great earthquake of March
27 1964. The earthquake set off a giant
landslide that wrenched houses apart.
Half a square mile of flat-lying headland
surged towards the sea. At the same time,
along 400 miles of coast, Alaskans were
battling with falling buildings, tsunamis
and fires.

**The beautiful, ancient hill-top
village of Calabritto, southern Italy**
(below), shattered by the earthquake of
November 23 1980. Houses stacked one
upon another like a honeycomb, built from
rubble and poor mortar, are particularly
vulnerable when the ground begins to shake.
The damage is worst on the ridge crest.
Before the earthquake the skyline was
castellated: destruction has razed every
building to the ground.

had been torn apart as it had surged and crumbled toward the
sea. Some of the residents had lost their lives in the crevasses of
Turnagain Heights. Others had had extraordinary escapes as the
fissures had opened and closed around them.

Elsewhere in the city, people were thrown off their feet, furniture was smashed, and at the city's airport the concrete control
tower had been felled like a tree. A great crack had torn through
an elementary school, destroying the building as one section
dropped 6m (20ft). But this was not just Anchorage's disaster.
Towns and villages had been destroyed for 400 miles up and down
the coast. The year was 1964.

Disaster in Italy
At 7.34pm the mountain villages of Basilicata, west of Naples,
received a great shaking as the earth began to tremble and judder.
In the city of Naples, some 60km (40 miles) from the center of the
earthquake, a few of the older rundown tenement buildings crumbled and fell. At first it was impossible to discover what had
happened in the mountains to the east. Roads were blocked and
telephone lines down, but by the following morning it was clear
that there had been a major catastrophe. It was the ancient
centers of the villages which had been most grievously injured, for

most of the damage was restricted to the cluster of older buildings. The crude rubble walls had simply disintegrated, bringing the roof timbers and heavy pantiles crashing down. The tall houses and narrow streets left nowhere to flee. The centers of villages like Sant Angelo dei Lombardi, Calitri, Pescopagano and Calabritto lay in ruins as if smashed from above. The stones of the houses had returned to nature. The villages that once looked from a distance like great castles with angular turrets, now seemed more like rounded, boulder-strewn hilltops.

The new buildings on the outskirts of the old towns were less affected, so it was the peasant farmers, and the elderly in their ancient houses who suffered the worst losses, as well as the priests and the shopkeepers, who sustained the old life.

It took many days of searching through the chaos of the narrow village streets to establish that more than 3,000 people were killed that evening. For those who survived it was to be a miserable winter; a disorganized recovery program, which often meant camping out in the rain and the snow. Several of these beautiful remote villages, already hard-hit by a move to the cities, would probably never recover from the earthquake. The year was 1980.

A sea of mud

The eruption of Nevado del Ruiz, the northernmost volcano of the Andean chain, had begun at 3.05pm with a small explosion. But it was not until 9pm that the volcano entered its paroxysmal phase, with a series of hot ashflows pouring out from the volcano's crater. Ash and boulders were thrown into the air in a column rising up to 11km (7 miles) high, raining stones on some farms close to the volcano. At 5pm, soon after the eruption had started, a meeting of Government geologists and seismologists discussed the emergency, and it was proposed that several towns including Armero should be evacuated because of the threat of volcanic mudflows or lahars. After the more explosive main eruption had begun at 9pm, attempts were made to contact the town but these proved unsuccessful.

The hot ashflows had scoured and melted part of the icesheet that flanked the volcano, and the torrents of water had combined with volcanic ash to form mudflows which poured down the peripheral river valleys. Shortly before midnight, the first of a series of great waves of mud broke out of the narrow ravine of the Lagunillas River to spread out over the plain where Armero was situated. As the first waves of mud arrived, people fled upstairs, but the foundations of their houses were pulled from underneath them. The mudflows had split in two, leaving a mainstreet highway almost untouched. Many people tried to flee with the relentless tide of mud running at their heels. Some people were caught by great eddies and then swept to the sides of the current. Others on the edge of the town managed to race each successive wave. Most were trapped in the falling houses, or overwhelmed by the mud, which had a consistency of wet cement. Ninety percent of the townspeople were killed, buried in up to 3.5m (11ft) of the volcanic mudslide. In all, 23,000 people were killed that night.

A fortunate survivor
from the town of Armero, rescued from the flotsam of the volcanic mudslides that poured down from the volcano of Nevado del Ruiz, after an eruption on the evening of November 13 1985. Swept from their beds in a wave of abrasive mud, 20,000 townspeople lay buried amidst the ruins of their houses in a valley infilled with a new, thick layer of sediment.

The threat of mudslides had already been identified and their paths defined many months before the volcano erupted. If only on that night of November 13, 1985, an evacuation had been successfully ordered, then the people of Armero would have been saved.

Total disaster

At 3.42am, an enormous earthquake originating beneath the city smashed into the dull apartment buildings of Tangshan. This was no simple rolling wave that gradually built up to a crescendo. It was an explosion in the earth, as though the city and its buildings had been hit by a giant hammer. The buildings were crude, a few stories high, cheap standard housing thrown up in enormous numbers to house the industrial workers of this large city of a million people. No thought had been given to earthquakes in their construction, because no earthquakes had been recorded in this region. The damage was almost total, and in its effects, beyond comprehension. The suddenness of the shaking caught most people in their beds – there was no time to rise and flee. The entire city – university, schools, factories – was levelled. Statistics are numbing. This was the century's worst earthquake disaster. Only one house or apartment in 50 survived the terrible shaking. Ten thousand large industrial smokestacks made of brick and concrete were felled. Only one factory in 10 was not destroyed. Of 28 trains passing through the city, seven were overturned and many of the others damaged and derailed. All four city hospitals were destroyed.

But the damage was not just to the buildings and equipment. The death toll was frightful. At one large locomotive factory nearly 2,000 of the 7,768 employees were killed. Of those working on the night shift, almost half died. More than 1,000 of the students and teachers at the Tangshan Institute of Mining and Metallurgy died. The infrastructure of the city, the pipelines, drains, and cables were smashed. The fault that set off the earthquake emerged at the surface, slicing through the center of the city for 10km (6 miles), offsetting canals, railway lines, and buildings by up to 2m (7ft).

The following evening, 16 hours after the main shock, a great aftershock occurred, destroying some of the few structures still standing after the main shock, and finally destroying the 800m (2625ft) Luanho Bridge. It might be thought that the luckiest people that night were the 30,000 miners on nightshift, who suffered few casualties, although they could not be brought up for two days. But their luck in surviving was overshadowed by the tragedy of finding their homes and families destroyed. In little more than a minute a quarter of a million people had died.

The destruction was so total, the communications systems so shattered, that news of the disaster arrived in Beijing some hours after the shock, carried by a motorist. The year was 1976.

Rebuilding begins in the city of Tangshan – almost completely destroyed in the early-morning earthquake of July 28 1976. Only the strongest buildings even half-survived the terrible shaking and a quarter of a million people died in the ruins.

Forces beyond morality

At all these places, at all these moments, time stood still. Every detail of the commonplace and the everyday would be imprinted on the memory of those who survived or of those who came after to discover the devastation. At St. Pierre, the cloud of fire consumed families sitting at the breakfast table; at Tangshan most of those who died had hardly time enough to wake.

Earthquakes and volcanic eruptions, the storms of our planet Earth, are no respecters of holy hours, sleeping hours, meal times; no respecters of privacy or families, houses or churches. For every earthquake of which it has been said, "We were lucky that it did not come later, when all the children were at school, when all the families were in bed, when all the people were in the cinema," there have been earthquakes that have arrived to destroy a church in the middle of a service, to demolish a shopping center at the busiest time of the day. For every volcanic eruption for which it has been said, "We were lucky that the lava did not pass through the town," there have been volcanic mudslides which destroyed communities located in the fertile mountainside valleys. When an earthquake or an eruption seems kindly, overthrowing buildings when the people are working in the fields, or destroying schools when the children are on vacation, it is possible to find amidst the ruins the footsteps of providence. Only when the destruction is as complete as at Tangshan are we brought face to face with the darker side of the natural world. Yet we persist in formulating interpretations, good and bad, with regard to forces almost beyond human comprehension – forces which operate outside human time frames, forces beyond morality.

Perhaps no earthquake caused a deeper disquiet about man's relationship with the universe than the one which destroyed the beautiful city of Lisbon in the middle of church services. For some survivors, saved because they had not been attending church, it simply served to destroy their faith in God. The priests of other nations found material for sermons; the people of Lisbon had brought fate down upon their own heads by wrongdoing. Lisbon had been destroyed as a warning for other sinful cities.

At a distance there were others whose faith was shattered, not in God, but in the power of Newton's ordered and harmonious universe. What was human reason in the face of a natural world hellbent on anarchy, a world that seemed irrational and vengeful? The echoes of the Lisbon earthquake were felt throughout the latter half of the 18th century: the moral drawn contributed to the shift from rationalism to Romanticism – veneration for disordered but powerful manifestations of the natural world.

Was Lisbon destroyed because it was evil, was it destroyed as a warning for other cities, or because Nature was playing willful games? More than 200 years after the earthquake, the true explanation finally emerged as to why it was Lisbon that was "punished," and not Paris, or Amsterdam or London. The Portuguese city overlooks a great submarine rent in the ocean floor which marks the true boundary between Africa and Europe, and along which the continents are grinding together.

Life must go on: Mexico City after the 1985 earthquake. In the aftermath it is for the engineers, seismologists and politicans to assess the causes of the disaster, to learn from the mistakes and avoid a repetition of a tragedy that took 10,000 lives.

Even in the late 20th century it is commonplace to look for some meaning when an earthquake occurs. In Iran a damaging earthquake on January 16th 1979 heralded by only a few hours the departure of the Shah, and the victory of the Iranian revolution. A large earthquake which devastated the city of El Asnam in Algeria in 1980 came 26 years after the same city had been destroyed in an earlier earthquake, at the beginning of the war of independence from the French. To many of its inhabitants the earlier earthquake seemed just one part of the turmoil of the bloody conflict, as if it had been caused by "colonialism," but now in 1980 many of the houses destroyed were new apartment buildings, which had been the very symbol of the Socialist state and its commitment to the people. The Algerian Government had to act quickly and effectively to rehouse the survivors and provide new symbols of its authority.

It often happens that an earthquake raises political issues: in Mexico City, incompetent building and corruption were soon being blamed for the spectacular damage to new buildings. Yet more sober assessment was directed at considering just how extraordinary and unpredictable had been the effect of the ground shaking from the earthquake.

Humans find it hard to accept that something as devastating as an earthquake does not fit into a greater pattern. Many earthquake researchers have passed their entire careers attempting to prove that earthquakes were more common in the winter, early in the morning, or at times of stormy weather. The idea that there is some particular identifiable "earthquake weather" is still widely believed in many earthquake-ridden regions. The Greek philosopher Anaximander considered that earthquakes occurred when prolonged rainfall followed drought. The explorer Alexander von Humboldt thought that "one cannot deny that at the time of thunderstorms, the appearance of earthquakes is to be feared most." Aristotle believed that earthquake weather was hot and humid, because windlessness allowed the imprisoned air to burst from underground, and thereby to quake the earth. Large earthquakes were triggered by a particular alignment of the planets, according to a popular science journalist in England in the 1970s.

Earthquake weather may be sunny or wet, warm or cold. If there are particular patterns, or times, or coincidences when earthquakes or volcanoes shatter the stability of the ground, they have yet to be discovered.

Natural disasters punctuate history – every year as man appears to conquer the unknown, as the awe of the world diminishes, so such disasters become even stranger, even more sinister. Where are we further from the life and the pace of the natural world than in the heart of the city; and yet it is in the heart of the city, as with Mexico City in 1985, that an earthquake can cause the greatest destruction. A volcanic disaster is a simple act of God – but an earthquake is more sinister because the casualties are almost always caused by the fall of the works of men.

While earthquakes and volcanic eruptions do not come at an appointed time, ever after they take on special significance as a datum point, a landmark in a nation's history. Some earthquakes literally and metaphorically resonate across the globe: the eruption of Krakatoa in 1883, the great San Francisco earthquake of 1906, the great earthquake and fire at Tokyo in 1923. Unlike our ancestors we now understand the causes of earthquakes and volcanoes, but that does not lessen their power.

Yet scientific observations of earthquakes and volcanoes have in the past few decades solved many of the most troubling puzzles as to the causes and nature of these disturbances. With no choice in the matter, the planet on which we have evolved is an unstable planet, with a hot molten interior, and an outer skin which is periodically torn by convulsions. Even now there is a section of the Earth's outer crust, somewhere around the skin of the planet, close to breaking point, increasing in stress all the time. In a day, a week, a month, a year, it will finally break, tearing the rocks apart and setting off a vibration strong enough to topple buildings and bring chaos to the heart of some town or city. Even now there is a high-pressure molten magma bomb building up underneath some volcano, swelling the mountain, to culminate in an explosion that might punch a hole in the upper atmosphere or send avalanches of molten rock speeding down the mountainside. We are as powerless to interrupt these processes as a bird is to halt the wind. Our planet, no less than the oceans and the atmosphere, is subject to storms. Like a mariner preparing to go to sea, we ignore the possibility of Earth storms at our peril.

EARTHQUAKES

The destructive power of earthquakes: an awesome force that is no respecter of human achievement, devastating towns and villages and ripping through power and water supplies.

The unstable planet

The outside of an object does not always give a very good clue to the inside. This observation is one that geologists, mapping and collecting rocks from the Earth's surface, took more than a century to appreciate. The rock outcropping at the Earth's surface is no more typical of the planet than a pomegranate's shiny skin is of the deep red pulp inside. Nor can we simply tear a gap in the Earth's outer skin to expose the interior, as we can with a piece of fruit. Even the deepest drill hole in the world (in the Kola peninsula of the USSR) has reached a depth of only 12km (7.5 miles) after several years' work at enormous expense. That is the equivalent of only two hours' walk on the surface, and a mere five-hundredth of the distance to the Earth's center. If the Earth was an apple we would not even be halfway through the skin.

Earth's vibrations

As direct sampling is impossible, scientists have had to find subtle ways of looking into the Earth. Although the interior of the Earth cannot be visited, it can be imaged, in much the same way that X-rays and ultrasound can image the hidden interior of our bodies. The first images came from the study of the speed of vibrations as they passed right through the Earth's hidden interior. To understand the structure of the Earth, and why it generates earthquakes, we use earthquakes.

In the spring of 1889, a 27-year-old German physicist, Ernst von Rebeur-Paschwitz, had been carrying out measurements in Potsdam and Wilhelmshaven with a very sensitive instrument designed to measure the moon's gravitational pull, when he noticed a ripple in the record. He soon realized that this anomaly corresponded closely with the time of a large earthquake in Japan. Von Rebeur-Paschwitz was already suffering from a fatal illness and had only five years in which to propose his theories, and begin to carry out observations of earthquakes from all round the globe.

John Milne, British engineer and geologist, was born in 1850 in Liverpool and studied at Kings College, London and the Royal School of Mines. He worked in Newfoundland and Labrador as well as in northwest Arabia, before taking up a professorship at the Imperial University in Tokyo in 1875. When he eventually returned to England in 1895 he organized the first global network of seismic instruments.

His ideas were superseded by an English mechanical engineer and geologist, John Milne, who was teaching in the most earthquake-shaken of all nations – Japan. Milne had arrived in 1876 to become professor of geology and mining at Tokyo, and on his first night in Japan had been greeted by an earthquake. In 1880, after an earthquake had levelled parts of Yokohama, he called together his colleagues and formed the Seismological Society of Japan: the first organization anywhere dedicated to creating a science of earthquakes. One of the first objectives was to construct a self-recording instrument capable of preserving a record of ground movement. By 1893, with the help of English mechanical engineers also teaching in Tokyo, Milne had perfected the clockwork-powered Milne seismograph, which produced a record of vibrations on light-sensitive film. Within the next few years, Milne seismographs were installed in 40 locations around the globe, and their records returned to Milne, who had left Tokyo for the Isle of Wight in England in 1895.

Milne's Horizontal Pendulum Seismograph of 1899 (left). Light shines through a pinhole onto the pendulum and records a trace on photographic film.

One of the most earthquake-ridden regions on Earth (below) – Japan was battered by a series of quakes while Milne was in residence – this one at Biwajima Owari in 1891.

The vibrational energy of an earthquake radiates out from the fault in two distinct types and speeds of vibrations. **Primary or P waves** (1) (primary because they arrive first at the seismic recorder) are like sound waves in air and involve the compression and expansion of the material through which they travel. **Secondary or S waves** (2) are waves of shear that involve side-to-side motion like a vibrating guitar string. S waves cannot travel through a liquid or a gas. When P and S waves reach a boundary of some kind, like the ocean floor or the land surface, they generate lower frequency surface waves, which travel great distances – perhaps several times around the Earth – before subsiding. **Love waves** (3) are surface waves that involve side-to-side movement. **Rayleigh Waves** (4) move like waves on the sea, in a rolling motion. Surface waves decrease in power with depth – making mines safe in earthquakes.

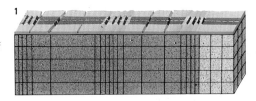

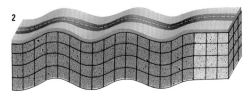

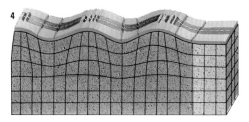

Only P waves from earthquakes pass through the Earth's liquid core, which casts a large S wave shadow. Increasing rock density with depth leads to increasing speeds; the shortest time-path through the Earth is a curve. The sudden density increase at the core-mantle boundary produces its own ring-shaped shadow.

1 Inner core
2 Core
3 Mantle
→ P waves
→ S waves
→ Surface waves

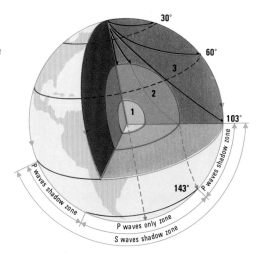

Milne discovered that the vibrations from a distant earthquake arrived in a series of separate batches, indicating that different types of vibrations traveled at different speeds. The greater the separation between the waves of different types (Milne called them condensational and distortional), the further away the earthquake. The method was identical to that used to calculate the distance of a storm from the time between the arrival of the lightning and the sound of the thunder. By ascertaining the distance of the earthquake from the records obtained from at least three widely separated seismic stations, it became possible to calculate the "epicenter" – the point at the Earth's surface below which the earthquake was actually located.

Before long, these different waves had been identified. The fastest are waves of compression or P waves, which move just like sound waves through the air. Next come the shear waves or S waves which move by sideways motion of the particles. Last of all there is a variety of surface waves like the waves of the sea, which move only along boundaries – principally the boundary between the rock and the air or water. While surface waves take the long route around the globe, P and S waves cut through the Earth's interior. What could these waves tell us about the material through which they journeyed?

Mapping the Earth's interior
In 1906 the former chief geologist of the Indian Geological Survey, fresh from studies of the Great Bengal earthquake of 1897, produced the results of his studies of the passage of seismic waves through the Earth. He showed that in the center of the planet there lay a spherical body or core which casts a seismic shadow on the opposite side of the Earth. In 1911 a German seismologist, Beno Gutenberg, worked out the exact shape of the core buried at a depth of almost 4,000km (2,500 miles), and showed that the core had to be molten, as shear waves could not pass through it.

Already, other significant layers were being defined. After studying the records of an earthquake in Croatia, Yugoslavia in 1909, the Yugoslav seismologist Andreiji Mohorovicić found that there was an important boundary between the lighter rocks of the crust and the dense rocks of the underlying mantle at depths of about 50km (30 miles). The same boundary, known as the Mohorovicić Discontinuity or more simply Moho, was subsequently found to occur at between 25 and 70km (15 and 43 miles) under the continents, and at depths of around 6km (4 miles) beneath the ocean floor.

Continued study of the records of distant earthquakes gradually began to flesh out other local boundaries within the crust and mantle, and even an inner solid core at the center of the molten core. With powerful computers, it became possible to map more complex three-dimensional structures in the earth from the passage of earthquake vibrations – a process of "tomography," identical to that employed in the body scanner found in hospitals. By placing seismic recorders around a volcano, it is possible to study how the vibrations from distant earthquakes pass through

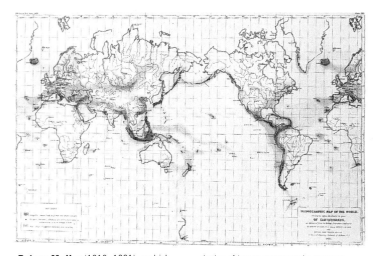

Robert Mallet (1810–1881), an Irish civil engineer, set out to construct a new science of earthquakes and traveled to the major libraries of Europe to collect all the information on past earthquakes. By 1857 he had constructed a map of earthquake geography for the whole world. The darker shades of brown represent the greatest concentrations of damaging earthquakes, which we now know lie along the plate boundaries. Incomplete only in the mid-oceans, Mallet's earthquake map could not be improved upon for a whole century.

the rocks beneath the volcano and hence define, from the absence of shear waves, the exact location and shape of a large chamber of molten rock or magma. From subtle variations in velocity of the earthquake waves passing right through the earth, the computer is able to map where the mantle is rising and where it is sinking.

Mapping the detailed structure of the crust through waiting for a local earthquake might take many decades. The use of man-made earthquakes began with dynamite charges in the search for oil in the 1920s. Today, earthquakes are made with large vibrating lorries on land, and powerful airguns at sea. The reflections of the artificial earthquakes from deep into the crust are processed with powerful computers, and a picture is produced as if the top of the Earth's crust, and its geology, had been made semitransparent. These techniques, all of which were developed from a century-old study of earthquakes, now provide the substance of a multi-billion-dollar oil prospecting industry, which has found many of the world's oil reservoirs hidden beneath great depths of water, or buried beneath thick covers of sediment.

Earthquake geography

The second important insight into understanding the behavior of our planet came from studying where earthquakes occur. From the earliest civilizations it has been known that some parts of the world are far more prone to earthquakes than others. The Greeks found their own city-states to be earthquake prone, as did the Romans, but the northern empire, stretching as far as Scotland, was notably less shaken by earthquakes. The Chinese always suffered earthquakes, but not as many as the Japanese, to whom earthquakes were almost an everyday occurrence. The Spanish colonies on the western coast of South America suffered extraordinarily large earthquakes which destroyed a number of the early settlements, but the towns on the east coast were rarely affected. Earthquakes were not a great problem for the colonists in North America, until settlements grew up out West in California.

In 1857 an Irish civil engineer, Robert Mallet, compiled information about earthquakes from across the globe onto a single map. He even included the evidence of submarine earthquakes felt by ships traversing the most important ocean trade routes. Generally the ship's crew thought they had hit a reef, until a sounding showed deep water. A number of such seaquakes, as they were called, were found around the center of the Atlantic Ocean. Mallet painted his map in different colors to show which areas had the most severe earthquakes. The map was not to be improved upon for a century.

At the beginning of the 20th century, after the spread of seismic recording instruments across the globe, researchers noticed that some earthquakes seemed to occur at depths as great as 700km (435 miles) down, far below the crust and well into the mantle. These deep earthquakes were restricted to certain narrow zones, in particular around the East Indies, and also beneath the "ring of fire," the zone of volcanoes that fringes the Pacific Ocean. In 1934 the Japanese seismologist Kiyoo Wadati made a detailed and accurate study of the deep earthquakes around Japan, and showed that they lay on an inclined plane, dipping into the earth. In 1954 an American seismologist, Hugo Benioff, showed that these planes intersected the Earth's surface at the deep ocean trenches, running parallel with the Dutch East Indies and fringing the Pacific coast.

From 1900 onward, evidence had been increasing that earthquakes were caused by the sudden breakage of the rocks along planar fractures – known as faults. A great improvement in understanding came with the construction of a global network of seismic instruments known as the World Wide Standardized Seismograph Network (or WWSSN). From 1960 this system produced a picture that finally improved on Mallet's map and indicated the pattern of earthquakes around the whole globe.

Along the center of the Atlantic Ocean, a range of submarine mountains was discovered, which started from the Arctic Ocean, and continued in two submerged mountain chains around the Antarctic Ocean, one passing into the Pacific and the second into the Indian Ocean. This range of mountains was found to be composed of very young volcanic rock. Volcanoes continued to erupt on the sea floor along the range, and even in certain places, such as Iceland, above the sea. By 1965 it had been discovered that the age of the rocks of the ocean floor increases very regularly in passing away from the ridge, dating back to about 150 million years at the edge of the continents fringing the Atlantic. Finally, the scraps of evidence provided by the earthquakes and the volcanoes were put together to make a simple story of how planet Earth behaved. The story was called plate tectonics.

| Key | ● Hot spots | ▲ Active volcanoes |

Plate tectonics

As earthquakes involve rock fracture, those areas with many earthquakes must involve large amounts of fracture. In areas without earthquakes the outer shell of the earth is not deforming and is effectively rigid. These rigid earthquake-free areas are known as plates. The plates include both the crust and the upper-most mantle, and are about 100km (62 miles) thick. Where one plate moves relative to the adjacent plate, there is a plate bound-ary, and it is the plate boundary which has all the rock fracture and the earthquakes. The zones of earthquakes around the world have helped to define about six major plates and a number of smaller ones.

Seismologists established that the boundaries between the plates fell into two broad types – zones where the plates were separating,

| | Earthquake areas | | | Plate boundaries |

1	South American Plate	**6**	Arabian Plate	**11**	Juan de Fuca Plate
2	African Plate	**7**	Antarctic Plate	**12**	North American Plate
3	Turkish-Aegean Plate	**8**	Indo-Australian Plate	**13**	Caribbean Plate
4	Eurasian Plate	**9**	Philippine Plate	**14**	Cocos Plate
5	Iranian Plate	**10**	Pacific Plate	**15**	Nazca Plate

Earth's rigid outer rind is broken into a number of tectonic plates, about 100km (62 miles) in thickness. These plates move at speeds of up to 10cm (4in) a year over an underlying layer of hot, almost molten rock, known as the asthenosphere, and are powered by massive sluggish currents in the Earth's mantle. The great majority of earthquakes, caused by the breakage of the rigid crust, occur along the boundaries of the plates, where they collide head-on or slide past one another. Volcanoes also form along plate boundaries, where rivers of molten rock pour out from the rising mantle or burn off from the sinking ocean crust. Isolated thermal upwellings may also cause volcanoes to form within the plates. Occasional rogue earthquakes also occur in the plate interiors.

Movements at the boundaries of
Earth's jostling crustal plates define four
types of seismically-active region, seen here
in cross section.

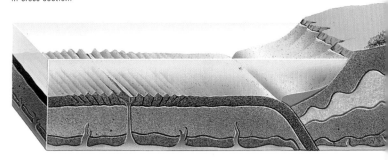

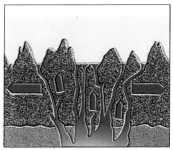

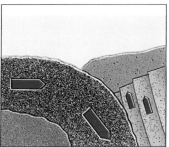

The spreading ridge: the extensional
plate boundary involves molten rock or
magma pouring out from the mantle to
solidify on the seafloor or underground. New
ocean crust is created which drifts away
from the spreading ridge. The thin hot crust
makes for small earthquakes.

The subduction zone: here, the old
ocean plate (the crust and underlying
mantle) sinks and bends back into the
mantle, forming an ocean trench and
melting at depth to create volcanoes. The
rocks are cold and hard, the faults large and
the earthquakes enormous.

and zones where the plates were colliding. There were a number of
clues as to what took place in the zone of plate separation, known
as the spreading ridge. First there was the evidence of the volcanoes found along the mid-Atlantic ridge, the fragments of mantle
rock sometimes carried up by volcanoes to the surface, as well as
old pieces of ocean crust found abandoned on land in old mountain ranges. Beneath the spreading ridge the mantle wells up and
begins to melt, as its melting point decreases with decreasing pressure. The molten rock, or magma, rises up toward the sea floor
and solidifies to fill up the gap between the separating plates.

In the zones of collision, the ocean plate goes back down into the
mantle again, causing a great depression or trench to form in the
sea floor and also setting off earthquakes along an inclined plane
down to depths of 700km (435 miles) as found by Wadati and
Benioff. This zone of earthquakes and downward-moving ocean
crust was termed the subduction zone. As the ocean crust goes
down it begins to melt, forming a line of volcanoes set back from
the ocean trench.

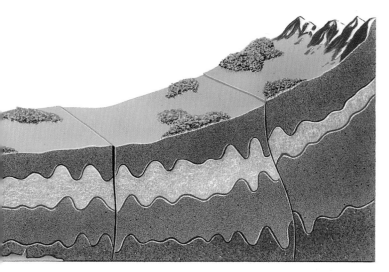

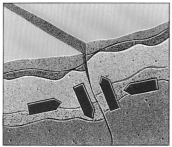

Transcurrent faults: in the continents, the longest faults (like the San Andreas) involve simple horizontal movement and may run for 1,000 miles. The accumulation of 100,000 major earthquakes and associated fault movements, over millions of years, can give offsets of hundreds of miles.

Collision zones: when continents collide, the crust piles up to form mountains. At the edge of the highlands, one section of continent rides over the lowlands. Sudden movements along reverse faults generate large earthquakes that can devastate the hillside villages.

Along some plate boundaries the plates slide past one another along a great fault zone, without colliding or separating. The most famous of such zones is the San Andreas Fault in California which is also the boundary between the American and Pacific plates. Where continents embedded in the plates collide with one another, there is no simple subduction zone but a chaos of crushed and collided crustal fragments which together produce mountain ranges – such as the Himalayas.

Whatever is driving these plates is hidden in the Earth's mantle. There are a number of locations where mantle rocks occur at the surface, where colliding continents have pinched some mantle material between them. Yet it is volcanoes themselves that provide the most important insights into the nature and behavior of the mantle. Volcanoes are no more than windows into the hidden interior of the planet. They offer in fact a glimpse of the real planet Earth – the material that is hidden beneath the thin skin of the crust, as the fruit is hidden beneath the rind. Volcanoes are the bursting through of the subterranean world to the surface.

To understand why planet Earth suffers volcanoes and earthquakes, and why the outer shell of the planet moves as rigid plates thousands of miles across, we need to unlearn our simple intuitions about the Earth. First, almost all the planet apart from a thin outer skin is remarkably hot. It is not quite a bubble of molten liquid but almost hot enough to melt, a sticky hot material, like partly cooled magma, right through to the central sphere which is liquid or at least has the properties of a liquid – the core. The hot sticky mantle flows like a liquid but very slowly – if you could hit it with a hammer it would seem like a solid. Some materials available at the Earth's surface have similar properties – pitch used on roads will break like a brittle solid, and yet if left for long enough will begin to flow. Another solid we are even more familiar with is ice. It will take a long time before an ice cube will flow away, but on a far larger scale nature has provided such an experiment for us to observe in the form of glaciers. Seen from a distance, the glacier seems to be made of a viscous liquid. Materials like ice and the mantle will flow on a large scale, over long periods of time.

If we can understand this great volume of hot mantle rock involved in sluggish flows – all held together by gravity – we can then in our imagination put the outer shell of the Earth back on

Glaciers provide good models for the hot materials of the Earth's mantle: ice-like mantle rock is a solid close to its melting point. Over long periods of time, such solids will flow – as this glacier – like a great tongue of sticky liquid, oozing down the mountain valley.

again. This outer shell is almost inert. Yet as the movements take place beneath it, inevitably they drag and pull and raise and lower the cooler, more rigid crustal skin of the Earth.

As the hot mantle material rises beneath the spreading ridges, it begins to melt. The deeper mantle thereby divides into two components – a melt or magma which rises toward the surface to form the ocean crust, and the material left behind by the melting which remains beneath the crust. The ocean crust and the underlying mantle pass down the subduction zone where they once again become mixed together in the mantle. Therefore the motor that drives the plates is not entirely hidden – the spreading ridges and subduction zones are the top end of a conveyor belt system which is driving the plates.

Around 95 percent of earthquakes take place along plate boundaries. Many of the world's volcanoes are located along spreading ridges in the oceans, or above subduction zones, as around the Pacific "ring of fire," passing from New Zealand via Japan, to the Aleutians, western United States and down through the Andes.

Yet there are many volcanoes which are not simply connected with plate boundaries. And a small proportion of earthquakes, termed intraplate earthquakes, occur in the middle of the plates.

Volcanoes are windows into the Earth's mantle. The gaping crater of 5458m- (18,000ft) high Mt Popocatepetl in Mexico gives every appearance of a bottomless pit.

Assembly-line volcanoes

In some places, away from plate boundaries, hot "mantle fountains" rise from deep in the mantle to burn their way to the surface as "hot-spot volcanoes". The Hawaiian islands in the central Pacific are built from volcanoes produced above the Earth's most powerful mantle fountain. As the plate moves westward, new volcanoes are born, creating new islands at the east end of the chain.

70 million years ago

The Emperor seamount chain marks the submerged volcanoes of the Hawaiian Islands as they existed then.

30 million years ago

A bend in the submerged island chain marks a change in direction of the Pacific plate movement.

Today

Intense volcanic activity continues at the eastern end of Hawaii, directly above the mantle fountain.

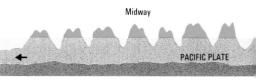

These volcanoes and earthquakes reveal that the plates at the surface are not always following exactly what is happening in the mantle beneath. In the middle of the Pacific plate the Hawaiian islands have all been built up by volcanoes formed from an enormous fountain of magma pouring upward from a great upwelling in the underlying mantle. The magma fountain is cutting a hole in the plate of ocean crust as it drifts over it, as a warm spring might bubble up through a moving ice floe. The chain of islands gets older toward the west, revealing that the Pacific plate is drifting westward over the mantle.

There are other regions in the middle of plates where smaller volcanic centers reflect fluctuations and local upwellings in the mantle. There are active volcanoes in northern Germany and central France, volcanoes in the middle of Africa, and in western North America. There have also been earthquakes in plate interiors – the largest earthquake in the past two centuries in continental USA was not, as might be supposed, in California, but far from a plate boundary in almost uninhabited Missouri in the winter of 1811-12. There were three great shocks – the last, on February 7 1812, was felt over the whole of the US east of the Rockies, caused enormous land-level changes around the Mississippi at the village of New Madrid, and even temporarily reversed the river flow, to the great surprise of the inhabitants.

The chapel of St Michel d'Aguiche in Le Puy, central France (right) is perched on the eroded remains of a lava pipe of a recent volcano.

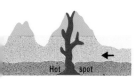

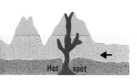

Hawaii

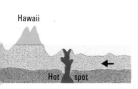

Such rogue intraplate earthquakes reveal that the plate interiors are not completely rigid. Plate boundaries in the continents are where movement is taking place today, and the zone of this movement itself changes with time. Like a Rubik's cube, a region at one period may be firmly bonded to the next, and then the boundary between the two becomes the site of movement. Large areas of the continents – much of Europe and North America – are riddled with old fault zones, which were once part of plate boundaries and formerly as seismically active as California.

Volcanoes and earthquakes do not always fit so neatly with the plates because the plates do not always fit so neatly with the movements of the mantle. The reason is that the motions in the mantle – the sluggish upwellings and undertows – do not gear through directly to the plates but operate according to friction drive. Imagine a series of plastic trays floating in a jacuzzi and you have some idea of the complexities of the relation of surface plates to the underlying motions, only scaled down ten million times, and speeded up another ten million.

Yet plate tectonics has made sense of the majority of earthquakes. Like any good scientific theory, it can also be used predictively. In the 20 years since the theory was formulated, a number of earthquakes have helped to fill in the gaps of plate boundaries where the theory predicted they should occur.

The causes of earthquakes

In normal circumstances – walking, driving, shopping, working – we do not give the stability of the Earth a moment's consideration. Unnoticed, unremarked, it merely provides the firm foundation for our buildings, our roads, even our graves. When the solid Earth begins to shudder and quake, it creates a deeprooted sense of doubt. Charles Darwin, caught in a giant earthquake in Chile in 1835 wrote, "A bad earthquake at once destroys our oldest associations – one second of time has created in the mind a strange idea of insecurity which hours of reflection would not have produced."

Before science, explanations for these Earth spasms turned to the observations of animals. The Algonquin Indians of North America saw the Earth as the back of a tortoise, stable and calm until suddenly disturbed as the creature shifted balance from one leg to another. In China, the Earth was supported by an ox which, having offered a long smooth ride, would suddenly switch the weight from shoulder to shoulder; the earthquake-prone Japanese claimed earthquakes were caused by the sudden wriggling and squirming of the *namazu* – a giant catfish, buried in the mud beneath the Earth. The fish was not so much vindictive as wild and anarchic – its movements could only be restrained by a god named Kashima with the aid of his massive magical stone. When the Gods were away, the catfish would play – an earthquake which destroyed the city of Edo (now Tokyo) in 1855 coincided with "the month without Gods", when Kashima was away on a pilgrimage to a distant shrine.

The Greek philosopher Aristotle sought to find less fantastic explanations. The Earth, he claimed, was honeycombed with caverns which sucked up the winds. When these winds became violently disturbed by internal fires they exploded out – as earthquakes and volcanoes. Philosophers after Aristotle all considered earthquakes as some kind of subterranean explosion. In the late

18th century, the new discoveries of electricity suggested that earthquakes might be electrical phenomena communicated over wide areas – the Earth had literally suffered a massive shock.

The problem with finding the true cause of earthquakes was very simple: in most regions that have suffered an earthquake there is nothing to see, apart from damaged buildings. While some older reports had claimed that the land had changed level and become cracked during an earthquake, these accounts were considered incredible. However, at the beginning of the 19th century, some detailed descriptions appeared of land movements in large earthquakes, made by more trusted observers. On June 16 1819, there was a great and damaging earthquake at the mouth of the River Indus, felt at distances across northern India up to 1,500km (930 miles) away. At the time of the earthquake, wide tracts of land around a low-lying area known as the Rann of Kutch became submerged, sinking by 4m (13ft). The fort of Sindree became completely overwhelmed by water, and had to be abandoned. At the same time an elevated mound up to 3m (10ft) in height and at least 80km (50 miles) in length formed on the edge of the subsided region.

Uplifted land

After a large earthquake on November 19 1822, which destroyed many towns along the coast of Chile, an English woman, Mrs Maria Graham, reported to the Geological Society of London that the coast had risen by several feet, leaving "beds of oysters, mussels and other shells adhering to the rocks on which they grew." A more celebrated observer was on hand for the great Chilean earthquake farther to the south at Concepción, on Feb 20 1835. Charles Darwin, with the captain of his ship the *Beagle*, visited the coast and found evidence of uplift of the land by as much as 3m (10ft).

After the destruction of downtown Tokyo (left) in 1855: a cynical print shows carpenters (top left corner) coming to the rescue of the beleaguered Namazu.

Charles Darwin came to study this rock platform (above) on the Arauco Peninsula in Chile, after it had been uplifted over a meter in the great earthquake of 1835.

The greatest geologist of the early 19th century – the Englishman Charles Lyell – used these observations to support his view that mountains were built from small amounts of uplift associated with individual earthquakes, repeated again and again over millions of years. However, so small was the number of earthquakes which showed such evidence of land-level changes, and so few were the accounts of reliable witnesses who had observed them, that the association of earthquakes with uplift became much disputed. Other later observers in Chile claimed they could find no lasting evidence of uplift from either the 1822 or 1835 earthquakes; by the end of the 19th century another great geologist, the Austrian Eduard Suess, argued that all Lyell's claims were mistaken and that there was no evidence for land movements in earthquakes.

However, as Suess was writing his geological theories, the Earth was busy creating earthquakes in support of Lyell's hypothesis – and also offering clues as to the cause of earthquakes themselves. While most of the major earthquakes in Japan originated beneath the sea, on the morning of October 28 1891 a devastating earthquake occurred in the Japanese interior which killed around 10,000 people, and destroyed 130,000 houses. A Japanese geologist, Bunjiro Koto, made a study of the affected area and found that it was traversed by a continuous great fault cutting through the landscape for 70-80km (45-50 miles). In the Neo valley, the fault ran north-south and cut through the low-lying land, dropping down one side by as much as 6m (20ft). In other places where the fault had swung almost to an east-west line, it formed a series of mounds, as if a giant mole had been burrowing through the fields. Here the fault had caused a horizontal movement, offsetting the sides of fields, roads and lines of trees by up to 5.5m (18ft). Flying in the face of all the scholarly opinion of his time Koto wrote: "In my opinion it can be confidently asserted that the sudden formation of the great fault of Neo was the actual cause of the earthquake."

Opinion was not going to be so easily shifted. It would take more earthquakes, and more detailed observation. On June 12 1897 there was a massive earthquake in Assam, northern India, and the head of the Indian Geological Survey, Richard Oldham, traveled to the affected area. He found enormous land deformations, with faults offset by more than 10m (33ft). However, the great tract that had suffered deformation suggested that the earthquake had been caused by movement along a fault underlying the whole region. But it was hard to gain adequate proof of such an idea, as the fault itself had not emerged at the surface.

The San Andreas Fault
On April 18 1906, a famous earthquake shattered the city of San Francisco. The earthquake was associated with displacement along a fault, the San Andreas Fault, that could be followed for more than 300km (186 miles) from San Juan Bautista, south of San José, north-northwest up to Point Arena. Wherever the fault cut some linear feature, such as a road, line of trees or fence, the two sides had become offset by up to 6m (20ft) with the west side of the fault moving to the north. A commission was set up by the

The earliest known photograph (above) of an earthquake fault, cutting through the Neo valley in Japan, and offsetting a road by 6m (20ft). The geologist Bunjiro Koto believed that the earthquake of October 28 1891 was caused by the fault movement.

Looking north along a series of low ridges (above) squeezed up out of the San Andreas Fault, which marks the boundary between the American and Pacific plates through central California. The Pacific plate (to the left of the picture) is moving towards the north, offsetting streams and causing earthquakes.

Strike-slip faults involving horizontal movements (above) are often hard to detect in an open landscape. Contemporary road markings are good indicators of displacements, as can be seen along this fault in southern California. Some faults continue to move after an earthquake – others move without earthquakes.

Californian state authorities to study every aspect of the earthquake and the faulting. They reported strange indications of movement – the fault had clipped the side of a barn at a ranch belonging to a Mr Skinner: "Under each of the east windows of the barn stood a pile of manure. Each pile is intact, sixteen and one half feet south of the window to which it belongs." The greatest damage in the earthquake was all close to the fault – buildings at Stanford University 10km (6 miles) from the fault were smashed while Berkeley, 20km (12 miles) away, was unscathed.

The chief scientist on the committee studying the San Francisco earthquake was a geophysicist named Harry Fielding Reid. A series of land surveys had been carried out across the San Andreas Fault in the 55 years prior to the earthquake, and Reid supervised a new survey to compare the results. Between the first and second surveys, and before the fault movement, Reid found that the whole landscape had become distorted, with the region to the west moving north relative to the east. After the earthquake, he found that the regional bending had become replaced by a distinct offset of around 6m (20ft) all along the line of the San Andreas Fault. From these observations Reid advanced his theory of elastic rebound: rocks gradually deform elastically over a wide region until the stress gets too great along the line of the fault – the weakest zone – then the fault breaks and the two sides rebound, causing the permanent fault displacement.

When all the evidence was put together, it was hard to dispute that movement on the fault had caused the earthquake. But could this be used to justify the argument that all earthquakes had a similar cause? Even after the apparently conclusive evidence of the 1906 San Francisco earthquake, there were still many geologists and seismologists prepared to argue that fault movements were the

Resting:
a road serves to mark the deformation that precedes a fault movement.

Build-up of stress:
as the two sides move, the intervening crust begins to deform.

Rupture:
when the stress is great enough, sudden movement takes place along a fault.

Resting:
fault movement relieves crustal deformation in "elastic rebound"

result, not the cause, of earthquakes. For a while it seemed impossible to prove that all small earthquakes buried deep in the crust could be shown to have emerged from fault movements. However, the conclusive evidence that all (or almost all) earthquakes are caused by the sudden displacement along a fault, came from observations based on Reid's model of elastic rebound. For an underground explosion such as an atom bomb test, the energy is emitted equally in all directions as a wave of compression. But the energy for natural earthquakes is released by a fault movement. The first wave is only a wave of compression, or *push*, for half the directions away from the source, and for the other half it is an opposite wave of dilatation, or *pull*. Detailed analysis of the seismic records from instruments spread all round even small earthquakes showed that elastic rebound had taken place along a deeply buried fault.

Measuring earthquakes

The earliest ways of measuring earthquake size were developed in order to classify over 1,000 earthquakes – several of them large and damaging – experienced in southern Italy toward the end of the 18th century. The scale was crude: earthquakes were simply divided into "slight, moderate, strong, and very strong." New scales of the felt effects of earthquakes were constructed in Italy and Switzerland at the end of the 19th century, but when the young physics graduate Charles F. Richter was put in charge of the Seismological Laboratory at Caltech, southern California, he found himself time and again at the wrong end of the telephone, answering calls from impatient newspapermen anxious for some simple facts about the frequent earthquakes around Los Angeles. A basic measure was required, which could be obtained from the trace of the earthquake collected on the seismic recorder.

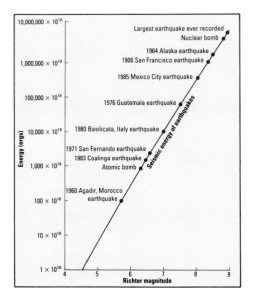

The stupendous energy-release from large earthquakes compares with even the most massive of man-made explosions. Energy increases logarithmically with Richter magnitude – hence, on the diagram, each vertical step involves a multiplication of 10 in energy released.

In seismic laboratories (right) information is fed in from distant seismic recorders, to provide a continuous record of ground vibration both on paper drums and on magnetic tapes. These provide a vital resource for understanding earthquakes.

The largest earthquakes of all occur along the shallow dipping faults of the subduction zones. The damage in Mexico City in 1985 (below) was caused by the prolonged shaking from the subduction zone earthquake of magnitude 8.1 off the Mexican coast, 400km away.

The problem is not a simple one. There are two variables: size at source, and distance from that source – a nearby whisper may seem louder than a distant scream. However, the length of time between the different earthquake waves provided a measure of the source distance, and from a measure of the recorded ground displacement it was possible to calculate the size of displacement as if the seismic recorder had been located exactly 100km (62 miles) from the earthquake. The logarithm of the displacement at 100 kilometers, as obtained on the Californian-built Caltech instrument, was the earthquake magitude.

The technique was soon exported to other regions of the world which had to calculate their own distance-amplitude relationships for their own types of instruments. The crust was found to be remarkably different in its ability to absorb seismic vibrations from one region to another. While the scale has no upper end, the highest magnitudes ever recorded have been 8.9. A whole series of different types of magnitude have now been devised, each of which measures a different part of the earthquake signature. After a large earthquake, it is common to hear a number of different magnitudes being quoted, partly because different observatories may not have completely comparable equipment or scales, but also because of local differences in the path taken by the vibrations in traveling from the earthquake to the instrument.

However, while magnitude is still widely used, in particular by newspapers anxious for a figure to fix on, the problems with it have been building up. In the science of seismology, magnitude is now tending to become displaced by a new measure of earthquake size, independent of the instrument used, the type of wave studied, or the ground beneath the instrument. This new scale is called Moment and is a true measure of energy released.

The realization that it was the sudden fracture of rocks along a fault that caused an earthquake now made sense of earthquake depths. Such breakages generally take place in the outermost shell, the crust of the Earth, because the rocks there are strong and brittle. Rock temperature increases by 25-40°C (45-72°F) for each kilometer (50-100°F per mile) below the surface, and at depths greater than about 20km (12.5 miles), the rocks become hot and ductile, and tend to bend rather than break. It is only in the subduction zones where the movement of cold rocks from close to the sea floor into the mantle allows earthquakes to occur at depths down to 700km (435 miles).

Small earthquakes come from small breakages, and large earthquakes from large breakages. The amount of displacement that takes place along the fault in a single movement is generally around one ten-thousandth of the length of the fault. The largest earthquakes known, such as those in southern Chile in 1960, and in Alaska in 1964, involved a fault 600km (370 miles) long moving about 20m (65ft). Because almost all earthquakes occur in the cold brittle rocks of the crust, a fault close to vertical, such as the San Andreas Fault, can only be 20km (12.5 miles) or less wide, though it may be 300km (186 miles) long (such as the section which slipped in the 1906 San Francisco earthquake). However, where a fault dips at a very shallow angle and is almost horizontal, it can be far wider. The largest earthquakes on planet Earth take place on such low-angle faults, found in association with subduction zones. Earthquakes such as those of Chile 1960 and Alaska 1964, as well as Assam 1897, involved large movements of up to 20m (65ft) on faults dipping at a shallow angle.

The orientation of the fault has important implications for the type of faulting and also the environment in which such faulting is to be found. The complete picture of the deformation of the crust of which fault movements provide the individual components is

A normal fault with about a meter (3ft) of displacement in El Asnam, Algeria in 1980, after the earthquake in the same year. The movement of the fault has scored distinct grooves (known as slickensides) on the fault plane. The steep dip (towards the camera) of the fault plane is indicative of a normal fault.

termed tectonics. Where the tectonics are compressional, as in regions of colliding continents, steeply dipping reverse faults may be common. Where the crust is being pulled apart, normal faults develop, dipping at about 60°. Where blocks are sliding past one another, there are strike-slip faults.

Almost all of the breakages that cause earthquakes are so small that the zone of fracture remains hidden deep underground. Only for the largest earthquakes involving the largest areas of fault movement, the fracture, starting perhaps 10km (6 miles) underground, may break through the crust to emerge or "daylight" at the surface.

Even after the identification of earthquakes with movements along faults, there were still some surprises. There are remarkably few earthquakes in which the fault at depth daylights at the surface to cause offsets along highways, fields and rivers. The fault at depth seems to get lost before it can break surface. Yet it is much more likely for a moderate-size normal fault or strike-slip fault to come through and crack the surface than for a reverse fault. In May 1983 there was an earthquake on a fault beneath the town of Coalinga, California, which caused great damage in the town. The fault was not even known to exist, but there was a major fold on the edge of town, which also contained an important oil reservoir. Fortunately, an earthquake three years previously in Algeria had shown that many reverse faults do not reach the surface but instead develop great folds on top of them. This gave a simple explanation for both the Coalinga earthquake and the Coalinga

The 1980 earthquake at El Asnam, Algeria was caused by the movement of a reverse fault. The hills in the background have advanced about 5m (16ft) along the steeply dipping fault, causing this ridge to form across a flat-lying field.

Mole-tracks: a characteristic and chaotic series of earth mounds, caused here by the collapse of the front of the El Asnam reverse fault. A farmer attempts to remove the painful evidence of the fault-scarp.

oilfield – the fold had even grown a little in the earthquake. Geologists were soon busy looking at many other folds in central California which had "suddenly" become the potential site of future earthquakes.

Earthquake magnitudes

As a simple rule, normal and strike-slip earthquakes will not crack the surface below about magnitude 6. The magnitude 6.8 Basilicata earthquake was a normal fault earthquake, but the evidence for faulting at the surface was only found after much searching. It had remained hidden in the snow-covered forested mountains. In contrast, the fault that caused the magnitude 7.8 Tangshan earthquake cut clean through the city center. Reverse fault earthquakes tend not to daylight below about magnitude 7.

For the low-angle reverse fault movement on a subduction zone, uplift and downwarping at the surface are not generally measured until the earthquake is greater than magnitude 8. The Lisbon earthquake, which was larger than magnitude 8, originated on a local subduction zone type overthrust about 100km (62 miles) offshore. Both the Alaska 1964 and Chile 1960 earthquakes were associated with up to 10m (33ft) uplift along the coast, and 2m (6.5 ft) of subsidence inland, over a length of 600km (373 miles). The Mexico 1985 earthquake of magnitude 8.1 was associated with only a small uplift of 10-20cm (4-8in).

Faults move when stress finally overcomes the friction. This movement relieves the stress. The faults are located in the brittle

Carlisle, northern England: a small, magnitude 4.5 earthquake in 1979 was strong enough to damage the weakest parts of buildings – the chimneys.

An energy release more than 10,000 times that at Carlisle, such as the earthquake of magnitude 7.5 in Guatemala (right) in 1976, causes severe damage to buildings.

crust, but the forces that cause the crust to become stressed originate from deep beneath the crust in the Earth's mantle. The mantle is involved in very slow motions (of a few inches each year) which drag at the overlying crust. The mantle has such momentum that it cannot be redirected except over geological time-scales – generally millions of years. Therefore individual fault movements in the brittle crust tend to recur again and again. This recurrence interval along a single fault is known as the earthquake cycle, i.e., the time between the fault movement and its repeat. It is determined by how fast the crust is being made to deform by the underlying mantle movements.

The earthquake cycle

The Earth's plates are moving relative to one another at speeds of a few inches each year. The movement of one plate relative to another takes place in sudden episodes of fault displacement along just one section of the boundary. After one complete earthquake cycle the plate boundary will have moved all along its length. The whole process constantly repeats itself.

Getting direct evidence of the earthquake cycle can come from the study of historical records – for example, in Alaska and the Aleutians the original Russian settlers recorded large earthquakes

over about 150 years, and in Chile large earthquakes have been recorded for 400 years since the foundation of the first Spanish settlements. The historical record of earthquakes in Europe and the Middle East extends for more than 1,000 years and in China for more than 2,000 years. Yet beyond this geologically short period (the earth is 4.6 billion years old) the only evidence remaining is preserved in the geology. Where fault movements have passed through to the surface they may fortuitously cut through deposits that can be dated, providing evidence of the recurrence of major earthquakes. Such techniques were most successfully used for the San Andreas Fault by a young graduate student Kerry Sieh who, in 1975, had deep trenches dug in a swamp north of Los Angeles. Using radiocarbon dating techniques, he found the ages of eight individual fault movements as far back as AD565. The repeat time of the big earthquake was between 55 and 275 years, with an average of 160 years. This proved that the earthquake cycle here was far from regular. The last such movement was in 1857, when a great earthquake hit an almost unpopulated central California. The next such fault movement is coming due.

In other parts of the world the earthquake cycle seems to run more like clockwork – big subduction zone earthquakes have occurred around Valparaiso in Chile approximately every 80 years for the past three centuries. Immediately after the earthquake, the chance of another big earthquake is very low, but this chance builds up through time until it becomes very high. Southern Chile and the Anchorage region of Alaska have several decades to wait for a renewed earthquake like 1960 or 1964, but regions on the edge of these subduction zone earthquakes have a high probability of a big quake. The repeat time of the big subduction zone earthquakes agrees with the plate tectonic theory. With plate movements of 10cm (4in) per year, an earthquake involving 10m (33ft) of movement should recur every century. Along the plate boundaries around the Pacific Ocean the recurrence interval, or earthquake cycle, is between 75 and 300 years. In that period every section of the subduction zone should have suffered a big earthquake, and the plate boundary will have moved a few yards all along its length. Away from plate boundaries, the overall rates at which faults move are much slower, and therefore the time interval between a fault movement and its repeat is much greater. This means that the historical record of big earthquakes is no longer sufficient to tell us which faults may be dangerous.

There are wide regions not on plate boundaries where the crust is being pulled apart or pushed together at rates one tenth or one hundredth of those found at plate boundaries. The earthquake cycle, or repeat time of individual fault movements, becomes correspondingly long – measured in thousands or tens of thousands of years. Such regions include the Basin and Range province of western USA (Arizona, Nevada, Utah, Idaho), much of the Middle East and Mediterranean regions, and also above the subduction zone in Japan. The Wasatch Fault is one of the most studied Basin and Range Faults, as it passes through Salt Lake

Far from any plate boundary, the town of Charleston, South Carolina, suffered grievous damage from a large earthquake in 1886. The nature of intraplate seismic upheavals is still not fully understood by scientists.

City, Utah. Geological evidence has suggested a major earthquake along this fault comes every 500-1,000 years. There has been no major earthquake since the area was settled more than a century ago, and further work continues to see if the next big earthquake is likely to be 50 or 500 years away.

Further into the interiors of the plates, where the crust is being deformed less than one hundredth as fast as at plate boundaries, the return period of major fault movements could be measured in thousands to hundreds of thousands of years. This means that the historical record of earthquakes probably forms only a tiny proportion of the whole earthquake cycle. Research focused on where the last big earthquakes occurred – as in New Madrid in the 1811-12 earthquakes and in Charleston, South Carolina in 1886 – has yet to find exactly why these large intraplate earthquakes happened where they happened. If one thing is almost certain it is that the next large intraplate earthquake in North America will occur somewhere else.

Controlling earthquakes

Having understood how earthquakes are caused, it is natural that attention should then have shifted to how these fault movements could be controlled. The belief that man could be lord over the earthquake culminated in the 1960s, but the story begins earlier.

In 1935 the great Hoover dam was built on the Colorado River, and as the Lake Mead reservoir began to fill, some tremors were felt in a region in which none had been known before. In 1939 when the reservoir was three quarters full the largest of the series occurred, a magnitude 5 earthquake which rattled through the city of Las Vegas.

The construction of the great Kariba dam on the Zambezi River in southern Africa was completed in 1958 and as the reservoir began to fill, the region was shaken by more than 2,000 tremors up to magnitude 5.8. At Koyna, near Bombay in western India, a similar dam was finished in 1962, and the reservoir was full by 1965. However, it was not until 1967 that earthquakes began to be felt. At the end of that year, on December 11, there was a magnitude 6.4 shock, which caused much damage to a neighboring village, involving 177 deaths and 2,300 injuries. Clearly more had to be known about this phenomenon, not least by reservoir authorities worried as to whether they might be held responsible.

Further clues about man's ability to cause earthquakes were found from pumping water down deep wells. From the beginning of 1962 the waste product of a factory manufacturing chemical weapons, located on the outskirts of Denver, Colorado, was disposed down a borehole nearly two miles deep. Soon after pumping began, a series of minor earthquakes were felt by residents of the Denver suburbs. All of these shocks were located around the bottom of the well. It was gradually realized that the pumping was causing the earthquakes, and eventually the waste disposal was stopped.

The opportunity to turn these observations into a controlled scientific experiment came in 1969 when experiments were undertaken at the Rangeley oil field, in northwestern Colorado. Water injection had been undertaken to aid oil recovery from the field since 1957, and now the water pressures at depths of around 1.5km (1 mile) were higher than those in the original oil reservoir. It was found to be possible to control the number of small earthquakes occurring around the base of the field – the number increasing when pressure was raised and rapidly decreasing when pressure was lowered.

It was clear, therefore, that increasing the pressure of the water, which could also act as a lubricant, helped trigger earthquakes. While the weight of the water in the reservoirs at Lake Mead, Kariba and Koyna might have assisted in the process, it was probably the water pressure along the fault plane that triggered the earthquakes. Yet the earthquakes themselves were also probably relieving tectonic stresses built up over very long periods, and would have occurred sometime. The water pressure merely brought that fault movement forward in time. It would take more than a clever law court to establish whether the earthquake was an act of God or an act of man.

The recognition that water pumped down boreholes could control fault movements suggested to some people that big faults, like the San Andreas Fault, could perhaps be controlled. The idea went like this: a series of deep boreholes would be drilled along the fault and all would be kept dry except for one in the middle, down which water would be pumped under high pressure. This would encourage the fault to move, but only along one short section. Then the same procedure would be followed for the neighboring section, and so on, until movement had been encouraged, section by section, along the whole length of the fault. The big earthquake

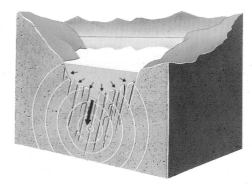

Earth tremors beneath reservoirs are due to increased water pressure, combined with the lubricating effects of water seepage into rock fractures (seen in cross-section behind a dam). In 1958, over 2,000 such quakes shook the newly-built Kariba dam on the Zambezi River, S. Africa (below).

would have been broken up into smaller quakes, and guided along the fault from one end to another, tightly controlled like a wild animal on a leash.

The idea seemed good, but was soon consigned to science fiction because of certain insuperable problems. First, earthquakes are triggered at depths of 5-15km (3-9.5 miles), out of reach of any but the most costly boreholes. Second, the magnitude scale is logarithmic – to release the energy of a typical San Francisco earthquake of magnitude 8 would require the controlled release of the energy equivalent of almost 3 million harmless magnitude 4 earthquakes. Third and most important, it is now known that many large earthquakes are triggered by smaller fault movements – they are in fact small sections of fault that just keep moving. Therefore, making one section move might well make the whole fault move. And then who would be held responsible? Earthquake science again and again has had to come up against political and social realities. It is good for the science that it constantly has to recognize that earthquakes are not some laboratory experiment, but disasters with the potential to destroy communities. Earthquake control cannot be the answer to the earthquake threat.

The effects of earthquakes

Imagine you have arrived in the town a few days after the earthquake has struck – it could be anywhere, from Italy to Japan. Across the land a vast and destructive vibration has torn down the houses and left them in ruins. The first impression is one of extraordinary ugliness. The finest buildings have been transformed into mounds of shapeless rubble. Mundane household possessions convey details of the catastrophe – a child's toy half-hidden beneath a fallen roof; a refrigerator oozing rotten food, smashed open on the former roadway; plaster blowing in the wind. Houses are as fragile as porcelain, humans as carelessly disposable as dolls.

The streets are blocked by piles of rubble that have spilt across the sidewalk. The interiors of houses have been cut open as though on display; shreds of wallpaper move in the breeze, an armchair totters at the edge of a crumpled carpet hanging from an upper floor. Here was a church, now no more than a heap of rubble and timbers, piled high within the ruins of the walls. Here was a modern multistory apartment building, the floors seemingly undamaged but pancaked together like crushed confectionery.

The aftermath of a major earthquake is chaotic and pathetic – amidst ugly ruins the survivors dejectedly search for their relatives and friends and collect their remaining possessions. In the Third World, as in Guatemala City following the terrible earthquake of 1976, the destruction can lead to complete destitution.

The damage has an air of casualness about it: pulling down an old house here, while its modern neighbor seems untouched; leveling one district of the town, while an adjacent precinct is unaffected. Why this apparent arbitrariness?

The resonating land

One fault differs from another, and the "noise" of a fault breaking is subtly different from one earthquake to another, just as breaking glass sounds different from breaking plywood. This "noise" of vibrations is the earthquake signature.

This sequence or train of vibrations rushes along at a few miles per second, the speed of an orbiting spacecraft; and the train becomes longer as some waves move faster than others, and as the vibrations themselves diminish in size.

The original length of the vibration train is determined by the length of the fault. A long fault takes several tens of seconds to break all along its length, and so the train of vibrations may last for more than a minute. For such earthquakes there is no real earthquake center – the whole fault is emitting vibrations, and close by, the shaking will be both very strong and long.

This vibrational train is itself affected by the materials at the Earth's surface – if these are made of solid rock, then the vibrations cause relatively small movements because the rock is strong, but where there is thick soil and sediment, the vibrations can become amplified through a process of resonance.

Resonance is the effect that enables opera singers to shatter wineglasses, and tides to reach more than 10m (33ft) in certain sea inlets. It is also an efficient way of felling a dead tree. Objects such as wineglasses, trees, and estuaries have certain fundamental periods (or notes) at which they vibrate. Tap a wineglass and it will sound this note. Let Caruso sing that note to the wineglass and every time it vibrates it accumulates more energy from the sound waves, until eventually it is vibrating so violently that it shatters. Push a dead tree again and again in time with its fundamental period and eventually it will break off. All those inlets that have high tidal ranges – such as the Bay of Fundy in Canada, and the Severn estuary in Britain – have periods of vibration which are very similar to the twice-daily rhythm of the tides themselves.

The ground can resonate in exactly the same way, absorbing one particular frequency of vibration and moving farther and farther with each new impulse. When different parts of the same town suffer very different earthquake effects, the explanation generally lies in some property of the material beneath the foundations. The potential for resonance had been noticed in a number of earthquakes, but it was the earthquake of September 19 1985 in Mexico which revealed its extraordinary implications.

The vibrations that traveled out from the breaking subduction zone under the east coast of Mexico had been moving for almost a minute before they arrived 400km (250 miles) away at Mexico City. The fault that moved measured at least 100km (62 miles) across and a second, larger fault had moved 26 seconds after the first. When the two trains of vibrations arrived at Mexico City,

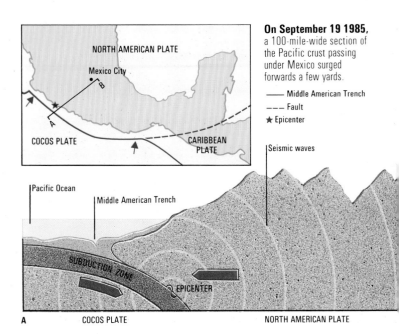

On September 19 1985, a 100-mile-wide section of the Pacific crust passing under Mexico surged forwards a few yards.

——— Middle American Trench
––– Fault
★ Epicenter

NORTH AMERICAN PLATE

Mexico City

COCOS PLATE

CARIBBEAN PLATE

Seismic waves

Pacific Ocean

Middle American Trench

SUBDUCTION ZONE

EPICENTER

A   COCOS PLATE   NORTH AMERICAN PLATE

one immediately followed the other to create an earthquake which lasted for more than three minutes. In a way which is not yet fully understood, the earthquake had an extremely large amount of energy concentrated in vibrations beating once every two seconds. Like white light or white noise, most earthquakes contain a whole range of pitches of vibration, but this earthquake contained the equivalent of a single bright color or a loud musical note. The earthquake waves are little different to sound waves, only this powerful vibration was beating once every two seconds, far below audible pitch.

Mexico City is built on a former lake bed, itself filled with volcanic silts and sands which settled gently at the lake bottom. Over the past 80 years the lake bed has been pumped for water, and as the water table has dropped, the ground surface has subsided – by up to 8m (26ft). This subsided lake bed is now in a curious part-hollow state in which the whole body of sediments is like a drum. The drum had been tuned by nature to a resonance of one beat every two seconds.

At 7.19am the earthquake began; the two-second rhythm, the pace of a funeral dirge, began building up in the lake-bed sediments, which bounced farther and farther with each new beat. The center of the old lake bed is also the center of Mexico City, where there were many tall buildings: few skyscrapers, but numerous offices, apartments, government buildings and hospitals of perhaps 10 or 15 stories. Buildings, like wineglasses, trees, or drums have a resonant frequency. These high-rise buildings tended to vibrate about once every two seconds. In a phenomenon termed double resonance, the buildings were tuned to the same

The first fault breakage was followed immediately by a second. The vibrations radiated out through the crust of Mexico, and in Mexico City, 250 miles away, they continued for several minutes.

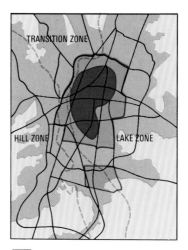

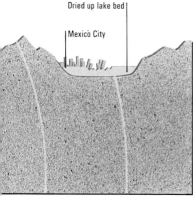

Dried up lake bed

Mexico City

NORTH AMERICAN PLATE   **B**

■ Greatest stuctural damage
■ Severe structural damage

The heart of the city was built over a lake bed, which pounded like a stretched drum, wrecking city center buildings.

TRANSITION ZONE

HILL ZONE   LAKE ZONE

pitch as the silt layers in the bowl-shaped lake bed.

On the outskirts of the city, where there was no lake-bed resonance, the shaking had caused little damage or alarm, yet in the center, many buildings were simply shaken to destruction with each fresh push from the earth.

A number of the world's great cities are built in drained lakes, or along the former swamp margins of rivers, where the problem of resonance of the ground and of buildings could be just as acute as in Mexico City. It may, however, take an earthquake to show that the resonance exists – in Mexico City the problem had already been recognized because a similar, but smaller, amplification of two-second vibrations had occurred in an earthquake in 1957.

Just as there are places where earthquake effects become amplified, so there are places where they are reduced. To escape from the shaking the simplest retreat is into the ground. Much of the punch of earthquake vibrations is released only at the surface: a few yards underground in a subway or a mine, there is rarely any damage, even in the largest earthquakes. Rapid transit systems in earthquake-prone regions such as San Francisco and Tokyo should be relatively safe places in which to ride out an earthquake.

Earthquake intensities
In order to develop some measure of the local effects of an earthquake, scales of intensity have been devised. These allow the shaking at a village in Greece to be simply compared with the damage in a small town in California. They also allow the effects of the earthquake to be mapped. Intensity scales were originally devised to be able to grade earthquakes according to their effects.

However, they have since been used primarily to show the variation of the shaking across a wide region. Intensity also allows us to reconstruct and map the effects of ancient earthquakes described in historical documents and to compare such earthquakes with those in our own time.

The most successful intensity scale was devised by an Italian seismologist, Guiseppe Mercalli, in 1902. Modern intensity scales have been adapted and readapted from Mercalli's original to try to make each intensity step of roughly equivalent size, and also to incorporate new types of measures. Most recently it was found that the shaking needed to spill objects from supermarket shelves was a useful and international intensity measure!

The Modified Mercalli Scale of Intensity (known as MMI) has 12 grades (expressed in Roman numerals), but it is easiest to explain it in simple terms from the even numbers alone:

Intensity II is felt by only a few people on the top floors of buildings.
Intensity IV is felt by almost everybody indoors but does no damage.
Intensity VI is felt by everybody indoors and outdoors and includes minor damage to old chimneys, ruined walls, etc.
Intensity VIII does general damage to poorly built masonry buildings.
Intensity X destroys most masonry structures.
Intensity XII involves total destruction.

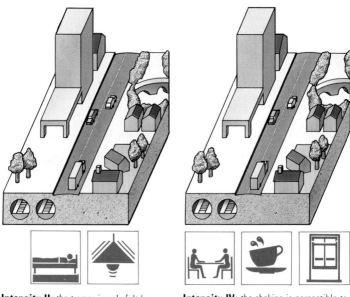

Intensity II: the tremor is only felt by people sitting or lying in the upper stories of buildings.

Intensity IV: the shaking is perceptible to almost everybody indoors. Windows and furniture rattle. Felt only by a few people outside. Resembles a passing train.

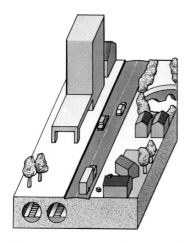

Intensity VI: felt by almost everyone including those walking out of doors. Unstable furniture overturned, weak walls and chimneys crack or break.

Intensity VIII: panic for all those indoors, many unreinforced masonry buildings badly damaged; almost all chimneys fall. Steering of cars affected.

Intensity X: destruction of most masonry buildings with their foundations; rivers burst over their banks; numerous landslides; many bridges destroyed.

Intensity XII: total destruction. Intense shock waves moving through the ground surface are clearly visible. Much distortion of lines of sight and level.

The intermediate intensity grades have intermediate intensity effects. The actual definitions are also quite long and complex; a 1931 definition of MMI VIII reads:

> Damage slight in specially designed structures; considerable in ordinary substantial buildings, with partial collapse; great in poorly built structures. Panel walls thrown out of frame structures. Fall of chimneys, factory stacks, columns, monuments, walls. Heavy furniture overturned. Sand and mud ejected in small amounts. Changes in well water. Persons driving cars disturbed.

From intensity VI and higher, as buildings begin to fall, we cannot actually gain an estimate of the strength of the shaking unless we know what condition the building was in prior to the earthquake. Earthquakes test building contractors as much as buildings. In major cities, especially in the third world, crowded tenement buildings sometimes collapse under their own weight, and even modern bridges and dams in Europe and North America have been known to collapse with no assistance from a shaking Earth.

In Iranian villages, where all the houses are built out of crude adobe (heavy mud and stones), they will all collapse at intensity VIII, and higher intensities cannot be assessed. In villages in Indonesia, where all the houses are made of wood, there may be no damage even at intensity X.

If you are in an earthquake there is more to notice as the vibration train rushes past than just the intensity. If the earthquake shaking goes on for a long time (over 20 seconds) then it is a very high-magnitude earthquake. At a distance a big earthquake will involve more of a rolling motion than a jarring shake. Like the storm swell of the Pacific at a distance from a storm, it is only the big, long period waves that keep rolling – the smaller waves (including the audible vibrations) all disappear with distance.

Most of the vibrational energy in an earthquake is at such low frequencies that you can only feel it, not hear it. If you are out in the open and you hear the earthquake, you are very close to it. Like an organ pipe or the string of a guitar, the lowest note the earthquake can sound is determined by the length of the instrument. In the case of an earthquake the instrument is the fault. For the longest faults of all, this lowest "note" may not only be completely inaudible but also cannot even be felt.

Around midday on November 1 1755, churchgoers in a cathedral in Germany were surprised to see ghostly shadows floating through the building as the chandeliers, hanging from long chains in the roof, began to swing lazily from side to side. About the same time, several farmers in southern England were amazed to see the water in their farmyard ponds rushing backward and forward and pouring over the banks. Villagers at Loch Lomond in Scotland were astounded to see the water in the lake, over the space of a few minutes, slowly retreating and then advancing once again high up the shores.

These bodies of water were simply responding and resonating to the passage of very long period waves, each one lasting for several minutes, generated by the giant earthquake offshore from Portugal which had just destroyed the city of Lisbon. The waves themselves could not be felt, but made large bodies of water resonate. Such waves in water masses at a distance from a great earthquake are known as *seiches*. Seiches from the Lisbon earthquake were noted all over northern and western Europe, as far as central Sweden. As news of the destruction of Lisbon did not reach north Europe for more than a week, these curious rural observations were at first inexplicable.

We now know that only the largest earthquakes – earthquakes over magnitude 8, such as those at Alaska in 1964 and Chile in 1960, generate these very long period waves that cause seiches. The largest earthquake can even make the whole earth resonate. Just as a large bell will only sound when struck by a heavy clapper, so Planet Earth may vibrate in an inaudible chime for a day or more after a great earthquake has rung.

Highly vulnerable, unreinforced adobe (rubble and dried mud) buildings in the village of Golbaf in Iran (above) have almost all been flattened by a magnitude 6.7 earthquake in 1981.

Old wooden buildings in Wakamori, Japan (left) remain almost untouched in the 1891 earthquake even though the shaking has been strong enough to cause great fissures in the roads.

Post-quake catastrophes

Earthquake damage is not just to buildings, but to all sorts of other lines of communication and supply which make up a modern town and city. Wooden buildings may be good at withstanding strong shaking, but in a crowded city there is an ever-present threat of fire. Like a city under siege, the earthquake both fractures the gas mains on which the fire can feed and cuts the water mains, making firefighting almost impossible.

In the famous San Francisco earthquake of 1906 it has been estimated that 80 percent of the destruction was caused not by the ground movement but by the fire that followed. This fire was not even triggered by the earthquake but by a woman attempting to cook a restorative breakfast on a damaged gas stove, four hours after the shock. The city, wounded by the quake, and with its water mains badly fractured, could not resist the inferno which destroyed most of San Francisco's business district. Yet while a quarter of a million people were made homeless by the earthquake and fire, the resilience to the original shaking of many of the city's wooden buildings meant there was a low death toll of only a few hundred persons.

On a fateful Saturday morning, September 1 1923, the citizens of Tokyo were not as lucky. A major earthquake centered 80km (50

miles) to the south ripped into Yokohama before reaching Tokyo. While only about one percent of Tokyo's buildings were severely damaged, mostly in the older downtown areas where the ground was swampy, two great areas of fire broke out in the city from overturned house stoves, igniting the wood-and-paper houses. The fire began to advance in two great fronts of flames on the Sumida River. As the frightened people fled with their possessions, they met in tangled confusion and panic on the bridges. There was no escape – the intense heat, and raging fire-winds carried sparks and cinders out over the river. The bridges too were made of wood, and soon more than 250 of them were alight.

Two thirds of the city, 300,000 buildings, had been destroyed in the uncontrollable fires that raged through the night. It was this raging inferno, not the earthquake, that took most of the 140,000 lives lost that day.

The lessons of Tokyo were obvious – the city had to be rebuilt without wood and with wider streets, for access and as firebreaks. Yet, as with all disasters, the needs of the people soon overtook the objectives of the planners. Ramshackle buildings were soon being constructed all over the city as the winter began to bite, and there was a shortage of labor for massive new housing projects. A law was passed that no building higher than six stories was to be

Onlookers watch powerless to intervene (left), as the Yurakucho district of Tokyo is consumed by fire after the earthquake of September 1 1923. More than 100,000 people were trapped and killed by the tremendous firestorm.

The center of the city of Fukui, Japan, (above) after the fire that followed the earthquake of June 28 1948. Only a few smoke-blackened concrete ruins remain.

allowed, but many earthquakes since have shown that the faith in simple concrete construction apparent in Tokyo after the 1923 earthquake was misplaced. Low-rise concrete buildings have become the tombs of countless innocent families in earthquakes since that time.

As cities are built with less and less wood the problem of major fires has decreased, although the trend toward the use of new plastics in architecture may well increase fire risk again. The crowded city center of Mexico City only avoided a raging fire after the September 19 1985 earthquake because there was no municipal gas supply. In Tangshan there was too little wood in the house construction for fires to break out and spread.

Oil refineries and gas and petroleum storage tanks are a relatively new source of fire hazard. At the town of Seward, Alaska, the Good Friday earthquake of 1964 ruptured the pipes at a major petroleum storage plant, and started a series of explosions and fires that looked, from a distance, like an atom bomb. The burning petroleum poured over the harbor area creating a sheet of flames across the water. The great waves that followed the earthquake carried burning debris deep into the town, leaving a burning high-water mark. The whole industrial area of the town was destroyed, including the railyards, powerplant and 26 giant petroleum tanks, but fortunately, as it was a Saturday, the docks were almost empty of workers and only 12 people were killed.

Fire hazard is only one among a number of secondary consequences of earthquakes. Another and potentially very serious problem is that of dam collapse. There has yet to be a major disaster although a number of small dams have collapsed in earthquakes. In the San Fernando earthquake of 1971, in a suburb of Los Angeles, the Lower Van Norman earth-fill dam came within a fraction of disaster as the crest of one half of the dam slipped into the reservoir. The water was prevented from overspilling only by a thin sliver of earth on the dam's outer edge. If the water had been a yard higher, or the shaking had continued a few more seconds the dam would have collapsed, flooding 80,000 people downstream in the San Fernando Valley.

In the San Francisco region, there are 226 dams with over half a million people living downstream from them. The spectacular and

A panoramic view of the wasteland (left) that was formerly San Francisco, after the all-consuming fire that followed the 1906 earthquake.

The Lower Van Norman dam (below) came within inches of collapse after the earth-fill suffered liquefaction in the 1971 San Fernando earthquake.

fragile-looking concrete arch dams have proved more resilient than the massive earthfill dams, yet among these, the modern understanding of the earthquake threat has been incorporated into their construction. It is probably only some of the older dams which are a genuine hazard.

One of the ways earth-fill dams collapse is by a process of lique-faction, when a water-saturated sandy soil takes on the properties of a quicksand after violent underground shaking. It was such material, beneath the Turnagain Heights in Anchorage Alaska, which allowed the great landslides to develop in the 1964 earth-quake. Liquefaction also caused great destruction to the water-front buildings in the San Francisco earthquake of 1906, and in the Valdivia earthquake of 1960.

Before and after: an enormous rock, mud and ice avalanche (right and far right), caused by a magnitude 7.7 subduction zone earthquake off Peru in 1970, which plunged 4,000m (13,000ft) from Mt Huascaran, burying the town of Yungay in 10m (33ft) of debris.

The ground vibration caused the sandy soils to liquefy during the 1964 earthquake at Niigata, Japan (below). As their foundations lost support, these otherwise undamaged apartment buildings slowly tilted and sank into the quicksand. One woman simply waited until the roof touched ground before disembarking.

The most remarkable liquefaction occurred in an earthquake in Niigata, Japan in 1964, when several apartment buildings slowly sank into the ground or overturned as the ground beneath lost all its strength. Even people sank into the quicksand up to their hips, although no one was swallowed up as the density of the liquefied ground was far greater than that of water. Often in earthquakes, water loaded with sand bursts out of the ground, showing that layers beneath the soil have become liquefied.

Liquefaction of the ground can also be a major cause of the landslides which are commonly triggered by large earthquakes. Such landslides may destroy houses, cut off power and telephone lines, and block roads, especially in mountainous areas, thereby preventing rescue teams from reaching stricken villages. Occasionally the landslides can be catastrophic in their own right. On May 31 1970 a section of the subduction zone moved beneath Peru generating a large earthquake which triggered a gigantic ice and rock slide high on the flanks of Mt Huascaran, 130km (81 miles) away. Millions of tons of debris moved down a mountain valley at racing car speeds, partly destroying the town of Ranrahirca, before splitting in two. One half continued on over a ridge to burst

down upon the village of Yungay, where the 30m (98ft) high wall of ice and rock engulfed the whole village, destroying everything and burying the buildings and people under 10m (33ft) of mud and boulders. Only a few inhabitants on the edge of the valley escaped to high ground. About 25,000 people had been killed in this single landslide, more than one third of the total casualties of the earthquake.

Landslides triggered by earthquakes can themselves cause secondary disasters. At Lituya Bay, in Alaska, a great rock slide triggered by a large earthquake on July 9 1958 plunged into the bay, causing a great wave that swept 1000ft up an opposite mountainside, carrying two fishing vessels out over the land into the ocean. Landslides underwater can also generate great waves – a rogue intraplate earthquake off the coast of Newfoundland, Canada on November 18 1929, set off a submarine slide, which moved for 500km (311 miles) out into the abyssal plains of the North Atlantic Ocean breaking many of the transatlantic submarine telegraph and telephone cables. At the same time the landslide set off a wave that inundated a number of villages along the Newfoundland coast, killing about 30 people.

Tsunamis

Most earthquake-induced waves are produced directly by the changes in the sea floor caused by the fault movement itself. Such waves were once called tidal waves, but are now known as *tsunamis* – from the Japanese for "a wave in the harbor". The large subduction zone earthquakes around the Pacific are some of the most important tsunami-creating earthquakes. In the Alaska 1964 earthquake and the Chile 1960 earthquake the sea floor was uplifted by up to 10m (33ft) as the fault moved, and the whole water mass of the oceans was uplifted along with the rock beneath. The collapse of the water caused an enormous disturbance which spread out across the Pacific.

Unlike wind-waves, tsunami waves involve the whole mass of the water right to the ocean floor and the speed of the wave is dependent on the ocean depth. Across the Pacific they travel at around 700kph (435mph) – the speed of a jet aircraft. The tsunami wave has a wavelength of more than 100km (62 miles) and a period of from five minutes to one hour. Out in the open ocean it is completely invisible with a height of only 20-30cm (8-12in). However, as it reaches the shore the wave slows down, banks up and can build to heights greater than 10m (33ft).

While most damage is caused to those shores close by the fault movement, just as Lisbon was attacked by a tsunami 40 minutes after being shattered by the earthquake, it is the effects of tsunamis

on the other side of an ocean which can be more remarkable – as they often appear to arrive completely out of the blue.

The orientation of the fault in the sea floor can cause the tsunami itself to become concentrated in one direction. The 1964 Alaskan earthquake tsunami clung to the west coast of North America, and around midnight the first wave arrived in Crescent City, north California. A warning had been issued, but as the first wave was only a few feet high many people returned to their homes. A much larger wave arrived 90 minutes later, destroying houses, starting a fire at an oil storage depot and killing 11 people.

The port of Hilo, the second largest city of the Hawaiian islands, faces northeast and sits at the end of a funnel-shaped and shelving inlet. On April 1 1946, an earthquake in the Aleutian islands set off a tsunami that hit Hilo five hours later, bursting over the waterfront to destroy buildings and vehicles and kill 96 people. The city set up a narrow zone of park along the harbor and reconstructed the buildings. Only 14 years later, the Great Chilean earthquake of May 22 1960 launched a tsunami that reached Hilo 15 hours later. It arrived in the middle of the night to overwhelm the downtown area with waves 12m (39ft) high, killing 61 people. A newer, larger waterfront park has now been constructed and a tsunami-warning service established around the Pacific, so that after a major earthquake, notice can be given of the possible arrival of a tsunami.

As the oceanic tsunami wave reaches the shallows (left) it rears up and breaks in a wall of water 10m (33ft) high. A graphic engraving of the tsunami that struck the Royal Mail ship 'La Plata' following an earthquake at St Thomas in the Virgin Islands in 1867.

A surreal juxtaposition of land and sea (above) after the tsunami. Boats thrown onto the quay at Seward, Alaska by the tsunami that followed the great Easter Friday Alaskan earthquake in 1964.

Designing for earthquakes

Just as the townspeople of Hilo finally learnt the moral of tsunamis, every severe earthquake provides lessons from which we can learn. The study of how and why buildings fall down offers insights into how buildings can be designed to withstand the shaking. The study of where landslides or tsunamis have destroyed communities can hope to offer clues as to where towns should be re-sited. The study of industrial facilities can hope to ensure better protection in new factories. After every major earthquake, a team of engineers investigates the areas of strongest shaking to inspect which buildings have withstood the shaking and which have not.

To assist this work, many earthquake-prone areas now have instruments called strong-motion accelerographs installed. Unlike ordinary seismic monitoring equipment, these do not run continuously but only when they are shaken, at which point they begin to record in great detail the complete earthquake signature of vibrations. These records can then be used to simulate, in advanced computer programs, the complete behavior of buildings in earthquakes. The records can also be used to drive shake-tables – hydraulically powered steel platforms on which models are constructed which are then shaken with either real or simulated earthquake records to see how they perform.

Why do brick houses fall down in earthquakes? Rather than wait for an earthquake, a corner of a house is built on an earthquake shake table at Imperial College, London (above). Seismologist Dr Willy Aspinall, from earthquake consultants Principia Mechanica, checks the brickwork before earthquakes of increasing intensity are applied to the table. The building eventually begins to crumble at the window corners (above right). At the strongest shaking (equivalent to the vibrations at the center of Tangshan, China in 1976) the whole structure is reduced to rubble (right).

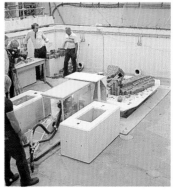

Yet as we are constantly devising new technologies, so there are always buildings and pieces of equipment which have never been tested. How do computer systems withstand earthquakes – how would a computer-controlled petrochemical refinery perform, how would a nuclear power station behave in a large earthquake? The Bhopal disaster in India and Chernobyl in the Soviet Ukraine have shown the terrible consequences of an accidental release from a toxic installation. What if that toxic release followed the chaos of a major earthquake?

When man lived in caves, or in simple wooden huts, earthquakes were rarely a problem. It is only as man builds larger, more complex structures that earthquakes take their toll. A commonly repeated slogan states that it is buildings that kill people not earthquakes. Earthquakes simply test buildings. Too many of them fail the tests. We ask our architects to provide a strong and secure enclosure but they assume, like us, that gravity will continue to tug steadily at the building like the ropes on a tent, and that the building will never have to suffer more buffeting and flexing than that provided by a strong wind.

Yet the art of earthquake-proof building is nothing remarkable – the techniques have been available for thousands of years. Building to withstand earthquakes is feasible – boats are constructed not

Earthquake-resistant architecture (left) is not always as striking as is the Transamerica pyramid in downtown San Francisco. In earthquake-prone regions from Japan to California, regulations state that all new high-rise buildings must be built to withstand vibrations. The ultimate test will come with a major earthquake.

Twice unlucky – El Asnam, Algeria, devastated by the October 1980 earthquake, had already been rebuilt after an earthquake in 1954. Now a new earthquake-proof city with a new name (Ech-Chelif) has risen from the ashes.

just to float, but to keep intact through the most terrible battering of waves and storms. If we all lived in the equivalent of beached boats, there would be few casualties from falling buildings in earthquakes.

There are some very simple rules to make earthquake-resistant buildings. First the simpler and more symmetrical the building the better. A box-shaped building is safer than a U- or L-shaped building in which different wings may vibrate at different periods. Large spaces in buildings are worse than smaller areas. Columns and walls should be simple and pass from foundation to roof. The building should also be ductile rather than brittle; steel in a building is very good for bending – brick structures tend to break. The most important rule of all is to lash the whole building together. Every component should be interwoven, so that nothing comes free. Often bridge spans, balconies and stairways are not properly attached to the rest of the structure.

Even today, not enough architects are fully schooled in earthquake design. The true test of the architect comes not with a test of knowledge but with an earthquake. Most earthquake-prone countries have building codes – supervising such codes is always a big problem because earthquake resistant-design costs money. Who is going to ensure that enough reinforcement bars have been used in the concrete and that these bars have been properly tied together? The interior of a well-built structure may never been seen again. Poorly built concrete beams are all too often made visible in the aftermath of an earthquake, when the building has fallen.

Design is only one part of the problem. Fixtures inside the building – computers, boilers, filing cabinets – should all be fixed down so they do not crash around inside the structure. Also it is most important to investigate the foundations for the possibility of liquefaction or resonance, and the likelihood of secondary hazards – landslides, tsunamis – all of these can be guarded against if they are thought about. Some towns, such as El Asnam in Algeria and Skopje in Yugoslavia, had to be hit by an earthquake twice in a few decades before the big lessons were learnt.

If large earthquakes happened to a city every year, they would be guarded against, just as we build to withstand strong winds. It is their infrequency that is the problem. The learning process does not seem to work; after an earthquake, instead of allowing evolution to operate – that is, to discover which buildings have survived and base rebuilding on those kind of structures – most villagers are happy to throw up their traditional houses once again, more interested in keeping out the rain and cold than in worrying about the disaster which they may thereby have passed onto their grandchildren. Now, at last, we are learning fast. In countries like Japan and Chile where big earthquakes are common and the earthquake threat is understood, many countermeasures have been taken. In a big subduction zone earthquake that hit the most populated part of central Chile on March 3 1985, architects and engineers schooled in earthquake-resistant design were pleased to see that almost all the new buildings survived nearly undamaged.

As man builds cities and high-rise buildings, he is showing how he rises above Nature – yet at one and the same time he is also offering up sacrifices to the forces of Nature. In the great post-war urban and industrial expansion, in particular in the third world, the crowded ports, the holiday hotel complexes, the new apartment buildings, and the oil refineries have often been built with little attention to the threat of earthquakes. As time passes and the lessons are there to be learnt, the lives lost in a major earthquake disaster become more the responsibility of the builders and planners than of the random violence of planet Earth.

Many people who have experienced a great earthquake from a safe vantage point have described a sense of elation, and excitement as they have been tossed around by the shaking. Earthquakes only provide a pleasurable opportunity to come face to face with the true power of a living planet when you know for sure that the building in which you are located has been properly designed. Will there come a day when, for all the citizens of California, Japan or Italy, earthquakes will seem no more than an infrequent fairground ride?

Earthquake Prediction

Dateline March 15 2053. *After several days of intense speculation, Earthquake Elizabeth has been predicted for tomorrow afternoon, along a central section of the San Andreas Fault. Schools are closed. Those who have a green clearout permit – invalids, the old and the young – are filling the freeways, heading out to room with friends in the east. The able men and women are staying behind, camping outside through the cool winter rain-storms. Their personal monitors are tuned in to the latest seismological count-down. Everyone knows what the various indicators being discussed mean: the radon count, the foreshock sequence, the strain-field, the shear-wave splitting and the P-wave velocity anomaly – in much the same way they used to know that a falling barometer meant rain. They also know what they have to do when the earthquake finally hits – they ought to, the schoolroom training has left its mark. The gas supplies have already been switched off, the city is settling back for a repeat of the 1995 shock, hoping that the lessons learnt will serve it well this time round. The prediction is only 40 percent, but 90 percent that it will be sometime in the next three days. If they have to wait, then so be it. Let's hope there's no repeat of the LA prediction of 2016 when the whole city shut down for three days and there was no earthquake.*

The shape of the future or science fiction? Earthquake prediction is a buzz at conferences, and in the scientific literature. It has the excitement of a new science, the earth sciences equivalent of the race to discover a cure for some terrible disease.

This smoked drum recorder (above) has just registered a local earthquake as the paper was changed. The study of small tremors along plate boundaries may give warning of an impending major earthquake. Big earthquakes are often preceded by such foreshocks.

Traditional prediction

For all the sense of breakneck discovery, earthquake prediction, the "science for the 21st century," is far older than science itself; as old as the stable settlements that developed in the earthquake-torn regions of the Middle East and China.

Homo sapiens has a great capacity to learn. Just as the ship-wrecked sailor will try to remember the portents of the storm, so the survivors of some village destroyed by earthquakes will try to recall the signs that preceded the shaking. Stories about the warning signs filtered through the countryside and were passed on to children. The earliest professional futurologists were the astrologers and soothsayers, and they were as much in demand 3,000 years ago as they are today. In the land of Persia, at the very heart of the great Alpine-Himalayan earthquake axis, the earliest known earthquake prediction was recorded eight centuries before the birth of Christ.

As we have seen, it is at the very moment that man creates a civilization, with its cities filled with temples and palaces, that he is also offering up sacrifices to the shaking Earth. As the culmination of all the civilizations and knowledge that had gone before, the Greeks, living in the midst of colliding continents, had much to fear from earthquakes. They began to write down their observations, a far more effective way of learning from the past than through the

Earthquakes were commonplace for the inhabitants of the Ancient World around the Eastern Mediterranean. Many of the most famous classical ruins, such as the Roman temples at Baalbeck, Lebanon (above) and the Doric Temple of Apollo in Corinth, Greece (left), are the result of strong earthquakes over the centuries.

braided strands of fact and fantasy that make up folklore.

The Greek philosopher Anaxagoras was said to have learnt to predict earthquakes from ancient Egyptian writings. Six centuries before Christ, Pherecydes, a tutor to Pythagoras, "when he had observed the water scooped up from an ever-flowing well, said that an earthquake was impending." The earthquake duly arrived three days later. About the same period the philosopher Anaximander of Miletus, told the people of the city of Lacedaemia to leave their houses and move out into the fields. As they waited, a great earthquake came to destroy their city.

The Roman general and natural historian Pliny the Elder, whose curiosity for the workings of the Earth storms lost him his life in the AD79 eruption of Vesuvius, noted four warnings of an earthquake. The first was a gentle trembling of buildings; the second was of excited animals; "even the birds do not remain sitting without fear." The third omen was that water in wells became cloudy and gained an unpleasant stench, the fourth concerned the formation of a curious fog: "either in the daytime or a little after sunset, in fine weather, the earthquake is preceded by a thin streak of cloud stretching over a wide space." In this, the most mysterious of the premonitory signs, Pliny was almost certainly copying the Greek philosopher Aristotle who believed that earthquakes were caused by the escape of the "pneuma," a spiritual vapor trapped in the Earth.

Of all these portents it is the second, the behavior of animals, which is the most curious. In the year 373BC a Greek historian reported that the inhabitants of the city of Helice, on the shores of the Gulf of Corinth, were astonished to see all the creatures of the city, the rats, snakes, weasels, even the worms and insects, scurrying out of the town. Five days later the city was destroyed in an earthquake and sank below the sea. Mere stories? The exodus of the animals sounds entirely fanciful, until one notices the same story constantly and independently repeated.

The French 18th century natural historian Le Comte de Buffon wrote, "Half an hour before the earth moves all animals are seized with terror; horses whinny, tear their halters and flee from the stalls; dogs bark, birds are terrified; rats and mice come out of holes." The philosopher and geographer Immanuel Kant reported that eight days before the Great Lisbon earthquake of 1755, the ground near Cadiz, on the coastline opposite the site of the earthquake, had been covered with worms that had crawled from the soil.

There are many other anecdotes of strange animal behavior before earthquakes, but such reports, without any possibility of verification, are not the stuff science is built on. The problem is that animals themselves make the poorest witnesses. With the advent of the new science of seismology, there was an attempt to collect these observations. Among the first earthquakes to be studied in detail were the damaging shocks in southern Italy in 1783. The naturalist Deodat de Dolomieu wrote, "The warning by animals of the approach of earthquakes is a singular phenomenon and ought to surprise us the more because we do not know

Could rattlesnakes warn us of a future earthquake in the Western USA? When the snakes – perhaps alarmed by vibrations or strange electric fields – emerged from the ground in midwinter in Haicheng, China in 1975, a major earthquake was successfully predicted.

through what senses they perceive it. All species sense it, especially dogs, geese and chickens. The howling of dogs in the streets of Messina was so loud that an order was issued to kill them."

Robert Mallet reported an Italian friend who had witnessed that "pigs . . . exhibited signs of depression and uneasiness ten days before an earthquake." After a damaging earthquake offshore from the border of Italy and France in 1887, the great Italian seismologist Mercalli, having sent out questionnaires on the earthquake to prominent and reliable citizens in the towns affected, was so overwhelmed with accounts of animals that he published a paper detailing those observations: recording that in 130 locations "a condition of unrest and fear among domestic animals was noted which expressed itself in unusual cries, restlessness, flying by fowl, attempts to flee into the open, etc., generally a few minutes before the earthquake."

After the invention of seismic recorders, asking people what they saw or felt before an earthquake passed out of fashion. Seismologists had finally created a science freed from the problems and delusions of human memory. But it was not just that seismologists were no longer interested. The whole western world was changing. People were moving from the country into the cities. How many of the inhabitants of Brooklyn or Chelsea could tell you whether the well-water was unusually cloudy? The folk memory, the lore of the countryside, has been replaced by the memory of newscasters and journalists – people whose job it is to find what is new, not tradition, folklore, old customs. Only in one country were the traditions of the past so strong that the old ways and beliefs were uninterrupted by the new science. That country was China.

China is a country prone to infrequent but devastating earthquakes. It also has the most enduring civilization anywhere. The two have worked together to sustain traditional earthquake prediction. The techniques employed are not so different from those described by Pliny the Elder.

More than three quarters of China's billion population still work on the land. In certain regions suspected as being liable to earthquakes, the people in the countryside were told to look out for changes in the level of wells, evidence of cloudiness or bubbling in the water, note down tiny shocks and keep observations of strange animal behavior. These observations were passed onto local officials, who in turn passed them onto Seismological Brigades who themselves carried out their own observations of changes in land-level, micro-earthquakes, and the levels of the gas radon issuing from the ground. (Radon, the product of natural uranium in the rocks of the crust, appears to be squeezed out of rocks as they begin to deform prior to an earthquake.)

The best predicted major earthquake was that in Haicheng, China on February 4 1975. The successful prediction was partly because of the local awareness of the problem but largely because the earthquake heralded itself so well. In the months leading up to

the quake there were reports of ground tilting, extraordinary animal behavior (including the emergence of hibernating snakes from their burrows to freeze to death in the cold), frequent tremors and natural water fountains. These strange phenomena reached a crescendo 12 hours before the earthquake, prompting the authorities to evacuate the city in time to save almost every life.

Yet the Chinese experience has also shown the limitations of the traditional methods. Abnormal animal behavior was only noticed in 10 Chinese earthquakes this century, and in only four was the significance of the behavior recognized before the shock. The great success of Haicheng became overshadowed within only three years by the terrible tragedy in 1976 at Tangshan. After Tangshan seismologists searched through the records of wells and found that various precursors had occurred but were too small and too vague to warrant a full-scale prediction. The Chinese have shown that the traditional forms of prediction may have their place, but cannot offer anything other than a partial solution.

Earthquake prediction saved the lives of thousands in Haicheng, China in 1975. The euphoria was short-lived. Only one year later workers were clearing the rubble in search of survivors from the devastated city of Tangshan.

Seismic gaps

As Chinese traditional methods were being tested, after many decades of hostility Western scientists were beginning to re-assess the possibilities of prediction. Before 1970, without a theory as to why the Earth suffered earthquakes, scientists had been on the defensive, pouring scorn on prediction as pure superstition. After plate tectonics, there was a theory that explained why most earthquakes occurred where they did, and also what caused them. Scientists therefore had the confidence to tackle new problems.

The theory of plate tectonics itself offered some of the most important insights. Along the plate boundaries the recurrence of large fault movements could be measured by the earthquake cycle, the return period of the same large earthquake. Within a single cycle the boundary moved a few feet everywhere along its whole length, in a series of individual fault movements. With a complete knowledge of when individual sections of the boundary had moved in the past, it was possible to identify those sections most likely to move next. These sections were termed seismic gaps.

Around the Pacific, a number of seismic gaps have been identified. There is, for example, a subduction zone under the southwest of Honshu, Japan. The whole subduction zone beneath the island moved in 1854, and two thirds of it moved in two large earthquakes in 1944 and 1946. The remaining one third at the eastern end passing through the Gulf of Suraga is therefore a zone at which a major earthquake (known as the Nankai earthquake) is highly likely. An enormous amount of research has been undertaken to try to refine this prediction – the area that will be affected by the earthquake is a highly populated and industrialized region to the southwest of Tokyo and Yokohama.

A view of the Gulf of Suraga, Honshu Island, Japan, taken from the Space Shuttle. From the pattern of historical earthquakes along the subduction zone that passes under this region, seismologists have predicted that the Gulf is at present a seismic gap in which a major earthquake is due. Many large industrial towns are located here.

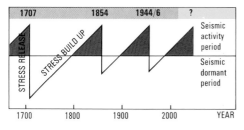

Stress builds up gradually on the subduction zone beneath Honshu, Japan, until relieved by a sudden earthquake-generating fault movement.

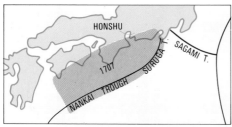

A massive earthquake in 1707 (preceded four years earlier by a smaller eastern shock) involved movement of the whole subduction zone.

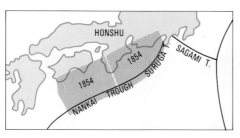

The whole western subduction zone moved again in two earthquakes in 1854, almost 150 years later. The eastern zone remained unbroken.

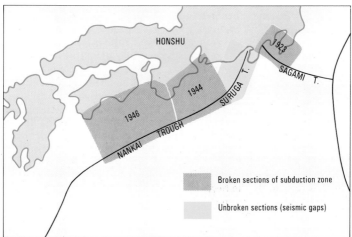

Broken sections of subduction zone

Unbroken sections (seismic gaps)

The eastern fault zone moved in 1923 to create the Great Tokyo earthquake. Most of the western subduction zone moved in two sections in 1944 and 1946. Japanese seismologists have predicted that the unbroken Suruga Trough segment of the fault zone will break next to create a large and damaging earthquake.

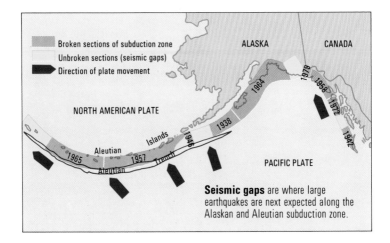

Broken sections of subduction zone
Unbroken sections (seismic gaps)
Direction of plate movement

ALASKA   CANADA

NORTH AMERICAN PLATE

Aleutian   Islands

Aleutian Trench

PACIFIC PLATE

Seismic gaps are where large earthquakes are next expected along the Alaskan and Aleutian subduction zone.

Other seismic gaps have been identified in Alaska and the Aleutian islands, both to the east of the section of the subduction zone that moved to cause the 1964 Alaska earthquake at Yakataga, and in the Shumagin islands farther to the west.

As time passes the probability that a gap will be closed by a large earthquake increases. In southern California along the section of the San Andreas Fault which last moved in 1857 there is a seismic gap slowly reaching maturity. Another large gap exists along the subduction zone beneath Peru, others have been shadowed across northern India, in Crete, and in the West Indies. In many cases the pattern of historical earthquakes is not known in sufficient detail to be able to define them precisely. It is only around the Pacific that the seismic cycle is so short that the pattern of earthquakes over the past 150 years can reveal definite seismic gaps. Of all the regions around the Pacific the most exciting work on the theory of seismic gaps has been undertaken in Mexico.

In 1977 a group of Japanese and American researchers working at the University of Texas noted that a previously recognized seismic gap along the southern coast of Mexico, adjacent to the province of Oaxaca, had since 1973 ceased to have a chatter of small shocks. They calculated that the gap was capable of being filled by an earthquake of about magnitude 7.5, but made no prediction of when such a shock might occur. In August 1978, a scientist from Caltech was visiting the Institute of Geophysics at Mexico City when she noticed records arriving of a second large tremor in the Oaxaca region. By the beginning of November she had gained the funding and the equipment to install a seven-station network of seismic recording instruments through Oaxaca. She was only just in time. A first series of small tremors ended in silence and then on November 28 a second group seemed to be heading toward the center of the gap. After a tantalizing 18 hours of silence the gap finally broke with a magnitude 7.8 shock which caused minor damage over a large region, but fortunately no fatalities. The seismic gap had been filled.

Freeway overpasses lie in ruins after the San Fernando, California, earthquake of 1971. Serious though this was, the earthquake predicted to occur along the south-central section of the San Andreas Fault will be 50 times more powerful.

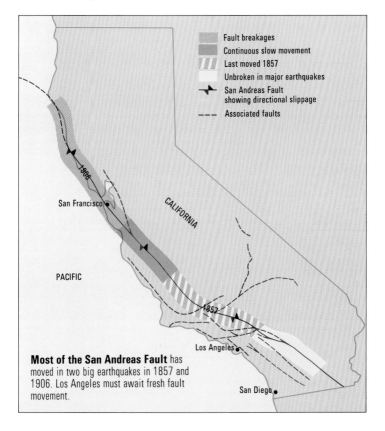

Fault breakages
Continuous slow movement
Last moved 1857
Unbroken in major earthquakes
San Andreas Fault showing directional slippage
Associated faults

CALIFORNIA

San Francisco

PACIFIC

1857

Los Angeles

San Diego

Most of the San Andreas Fault has moved in two big earthquakes in 1857 and 1906. Los Angeles must await fresh fault movement.

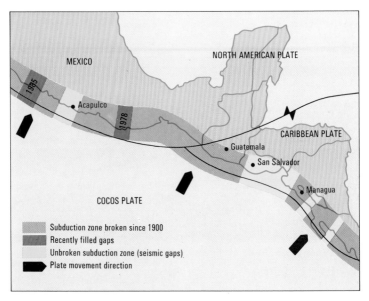

A series of segments at breaking point, revealed by the pattern of large subduction zone earthquakes along the coast of South America. One at Oaxaca was filled in 1978. The Michoacan seismic gap was filled in the 1985 Mexico City earthquake. Further to the east, San Salvador was looking vulnerable.

Another series of seismic gaps had been identified farther to the northwest along the Mexican subduction zone. To the west of Acapulco there lay the wide Guerrero gap, and beyond that again there was the Michoacan gap, which had been partly filled by an earthquake in 1981. In September 1985, in the region overlying the Guerrero gap, a network of 20 out of a total of 30 strong-motion instruments had been installed to catch the ground motion from the great Guerrero earthquake when it eventually arrived, so as to be able to use this information to improve earthquake-resistant building designs. However, on the morning of September 19 it was not the Guerrero gap but a major remaining gap at Michoacan that broke to cause the magnitude 8.1 earthquake which ripped into Mexico City. Like a trap set to catch a tiger, a lion had been caught instead. The Guerrero earthquake remains a sinister threat overhanging the city as the center is reconstructed.

Seismic gap theory provides the first form of earthquake prediction for relatively fast-moving plate boundaries. Yet many earthquakes occur off plate boundaries in regions where the earthquake cycle is too long to be retrieved from historical records. Even for plate boundaries, seismic gaps can only provide the first level of prediction – a second level of imminent warning is also required.

Watching for earthquake indicators

Surface monitoring is becoming very subtle. Cracking at depth may be detectable through observation of changes in the

A magnetometer (above) in a concrete pipe in central California, designed to detect subtle changes in the Earth's magnetic field that might herald an earthquake.

Buried underground in a tunnel, away from the extreme temperature changes at the surface, a strain gauge (above) records slow and minute changes as the rocks deform.

properties of shear waves passing through the crust; and an increase in volume, prior to fracture, may lead to a decrease in the velocity of compressional waves passing through the rock. Such changes in the property of the rocks of the crust may also affect the electrical properties, as may the emergence of trapped radon gas and changes in the level of the water table. Bulging can also be detected through accurate surveying measurements. Tiny earthquakes emitted as rocks start to crack can be recorded on seismic recorders which may detect a build-up of activity. A fourth type of premonitory warning occurs in areas where the ground is being continuously deformed, and it is marked by an *absence* of earth movement. Along many zones of earthquakes instruments pick up a constant chatter of small earthquakes – earthquakes which are relieving stress through a great volume of rock. When that chatter of earthquakes is switched off in an eerie seismic silence, a big earthquake may be about to follow.

The problem of all these indicators is how to interpret them. Since detailed observations have begun, the crust has sometimes been found to change its properties without a large earthquake following, and small shocks frequently occur without heralding a major earthquake. Radon anomalies can be caused by a raising of the water table due to high rainfall. The seismic silence along a previously active zone does, however, appear to be a good indicator of an ensuing major shock, but cannot help predict when it will occur.

It is relatively easy to make a prediction – it is far less easy to deliver that prediction effectively. Ancient earthquake predictors were not always believed, in particular if they required some undesirable remedy such as abandoning one's home. In Persia, the astrologer Abu Tahir Shirazi predicted an earthquake in the city of Tabriz in the year AD1042, and ran round trying to get the people to leave. However the citizens, who had felt many small earthquakes, ignored his warnings, to their own cost – 40,000 lost their lives when the earthquake came.

In 1549 in another region of Persia the local mayor attempted again without success to encourage the people of the towns to stay in the country overnight. Finding the night exceedingly cold, and doubting his own prediction, the mayor himself returned home to perish along with 3,000 other townspeople in the ensuing earthquake. Such stories sound completely credible. If we reflect on Anaximander and the city of Lacedaemia we want to know how he was so certain and why the citizens of that town were so trusting.

For every successful prediction there must have been dozens of unsuccessful ones. Earthquakes were often predicted because of the simple expectation that great events, whether political or planetary (such as an eclipse), should be associated with great earthquakes. An unsuccessful predictor would probably not try it again, if he had survived the wrath of those people whose lives he had perturbed.

Subtle changes in the distance between survey points, on opposite sides of an active fault, are measured with the aid of laser beams (above and right). As the strain increases during the build-up to fault breakage, the ground surface may rapidly deform, warning of an impending earthquake.

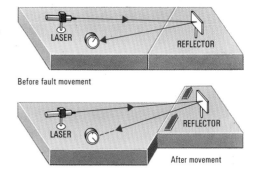

Before fault movement

After movement

Little has changed – the new scientific earthquake predictors are just beginning to learn the terrible responsibilities that their profession involves. The prediction of the earthquake around Oaxaca, Mexico in 1978 caused turmoil in the state, but the earthquake did at least take place. A well-publicized pseudo-scientific prediction by two US scientists of two giant earthquakes in Peru in 1981 caused pandemonium in that country. Seismologists may like to announce the problem as a way of getting funding, but it is not so pleasant for the people who actually live in in the danger areas. Crying wolf at earthquakes will undermine the serious research program as well as cause potentially more havoc than the earthquake itself.

Seismic gap theory itself is politically unpalatable. Residents of a known seismic gap might be cursed for decades by plunging property values, closing industries, and emigration. How does insurance operate when the risks of earthquakes become better known? To be useful, earthquake prediction has to be able to accurately pinpoint not just "where?" but most importantly "when?"

It is still too early to say how successful prediction can become. As the supply of large earthquakes is relatively infrequent we can only learn slowly. We cannot monitor every location where large earthquakes might occur, but even if we could, many of the phenomena that take place deep in the crust may not be detectable from

Like a hospital patient wired up to detect any change in body functions, the most earthquake-prone parts of planet Earth, such as here in California, are studded with seismic recorders monitoring the murmurings of the Earth. They may indicate a build-up in activity before the next big earthquake, or simply provide experience for subsequent predictions.

Tokyo fire department's special earthquake team (right) is a squad of 100 highly trained men. Come the earthquake, they will have to cope with all sorts of emergencies, from first-aid to fire and skyscraper rescue.

Earthquake education in Japan (top right) involves practise as well as theory. A Tokyo Fire Department ''earthquake truck'' invites citizens to experience the shaking in a magnitude 7 shock.

A sudden fault movement (bottom right) leads to more than just cracks in the highway!

surface observations. In the next decade we will hear more about attempted earthquake predictions, and observe how such predictions are tackled politically – do we just tell the emergency services, or risk launching a panic evacuation?

From what we have learnt so far, prediction will never provide anything other than part of the answer. We may concentrate all our efforts on one obvious fault, like the San Andreas Fault, and then a fault we didn't even know existed, like that beneath Coalinga, California, moves to cause a damaging earthquake. In Japan from the late '70s all attention was focused on the Tokai region to the south of Tokyo yet it was on the far side of Honshu island that a large magnitude 7.7 earthquake occurred in May 1983, killing 106 people.

Too much faith in prediction may also encourage complacency in protection. We could decide to put on a car seat belt only when we are about to have an accident – but it is more prudent to wear it all the time, just in case. Along the most active plate boundaries we have some idea of what to expect but very little of how the late 20th-century building boom will stand up to it all. Away from the known plate boundaries there are also the rogue earthquakes about which, despite years of research, we still know next to nothing, except that we are looking at a very small part of a process which may involve earthquake repeat times of up to one million years.

It is easy to be complacent – only worrying about earthquakes in areas where you know big earthquakes have occurred in the recent past. All eyes in the US are on California and Utah, when perhaps they should take a long hard look at Oregon, or even New Jersey. The Chinese cannot afford to focus research because they know big earthquakes occur almost anywhere across half their great country. A rogue earthquake the size of that in 1811-12 at New Madrid, Missouri, could cause extraordinary damage to cities in some continental interior in Europe or America, like the one in Tangshan, where no one had thought that earthquakes were a problem.

If there is one prediction that can be made with certainty, it is that earthquakes will continue to come in their unremitting, irregular supply. In some countries where the lessons of earthquake design should have been learnt, like Japan, Chile, California, we may hear of large earthquakes with relatively few casualties. In other third world nations where earthquake-resistant design was forgotten in the bid to house the millions flocking to the cities, there will be terrible disasters, with the possibility of even more casualties than in Tangshan.

And somewhere in the next few decades, there will be a significant rogue intraplate earthquake in the midst of the industrial nations of Europe, North America or Australia where it will be least expected.

VOLCANOES

Eruption of Mt Etna, 1971. Situated on the east coast of Sicily, Etna is the tallest active volcano in Europe. This eruption destroyed farmlands and threatened villages.

Mountains on fire

The 1779 eruption of Mt Vesuvius, across the Bay of Naples, Italy: a drawing by Piranesi. Mountains that suddenly explode into fire have always held a powerful fascination, feeding our myths with images of a fiery underworld.

Mountains of a strange symmetry, with smoke pouring from the top; mountains that after years of silence send avalanches of burning ash down their flanks, and huge black clouds to choke the countryside – no wonder that volcanoes in eruption have always evoked primitive emotions of awe and horror. If Greek and Roman civilization had not grown up in a region peppered with these strange and terrible mountains, how many myths would we lack – how many visions of a hot and hellish underworld?

Scientific understanding of volcanoes has not changed the simple explanations – volcanoes *are* the openings into the fiery underworld – the underworld of the Earth's mantle. Volcanoes are entirely unlike anything else in the natural world precisely because they represent conflict between the elements – fire from deep underground fighting with earth, air and water. The battle is between two very different worlds: the familiar world of the Earth's surface where the temperature varies within a range of about 100°C (180°F), where rocks are solid and brittle, and another hidden world of the Earth's interior where temperatures exceed 1,000°C (1,800°F), where rocks are red- or even white-hot, and flow like liquid. When the world of the mantle breaks through the tough outer skin of the planet to meet our own familiar world, the results can be dramatic.

The chemistry of magma

Why does the mantle break through where it does? It all depends on where the rocks at depth are molten. A small amount of liquid rock (magma), like a thin film between crystals, is widespread throughout the upper mantle; but to make large quantities of magma, special circumstances are required. Mantle rock is made from silicates (oxides of silicon), mixed with oxides of magnesium, calcium, iron and a whole cocktail of others – aluminum, sodium, titanium and many more. The rock will melt when, first, hot material from the deep rises in the mantle. As it rises, the pressure drops, and as the pressure drops, so the rock begins to melt.

The most common liquid to form from melting mantle is a basaltic magma. Basalt is a fine-grained stone, gray-black in color, which is the hardened crystalline form of the magma. Basaltic magma is the material that wells up along the mid-ocean spreading ridges to create new ocean crust. It is basalt that pours from the great volcanic islands of Hawaii and Iceland.

When the red-hot magma has broken through to the surface of Iceland, strange rivers run full of liquid rock, the molten interior flowing beneath the thin black laval skin.

The commonest basalts – those that form along the spreading ridges – are made up of large proportions of mantle melting, perhaps one part of magma for every five parts of mantle, and are termed *tholeiitic basalts*. When the mantle only melts to a small extent, perhaps 1 part in 20, it produces another kind of basalt, termed an *alkali basalt*, that forms isolated volcanoes, away from the boundaries of the plates, single small ocean islands or individual clusters of volcanoes in the middle of a continent.

The third common type of magma is formed down subduction zones. This is the region, as we have seen, where ocean crust is passing back down into the mantle. The ocean crust is full of water, and the mixture of water, ocean crust and mantle together melt to form an *andesitic* magma (indirectly named after the Andes) in which the magma is richer in silica than basalt.

There are hundreds of names given to different kinds of rocks

Cooling volcanic magma from within the Earth turns into a fine-grained stone of gray-black color. The hardened crystalline form of the magma is called basalt and may vary in structure. Here a thick mass of Alaskan basaltic magma begins to solidify at the margins. As it cools it grows polygonal contraction cracks, like drying mud, which advance inward, turning into columns.

formed from magma, but chemically magmas are fairly similar mixtures of silicates. The more silica in a magma, the lower will be the temperature at which it can remain a liquid, and also the more viscous it will be. Therefore, magmas rich in silica tend not to flow very fast or far. Granites are made from magma rich in silica that has been unable to flow even to the surface, and so has solidified in large crystals underground.

The other important component of the magma chemistry concerns gases dissolved in the magma – gases like steam, carbon dioxide and sulfur dioxide. Within the mantle, a small amount of these gases are trapped in and around the minerals. As the mantle begins to melt, the gases immediately join the liquid, so a small proportion of melting (as in an alkali basalt) makes gas-rich magmas. If, as in a tholeiitic basalt magma, there is a high proportion of melting, the gas will become diluted. However, magmas formed down subduction zones pick up the water, carbon dioxide and sulfates trapped in the ocean crust, and these andesitic, silica-rich magmas can be very gas-rich.

The making of volcanoes

When a pool of molten magma has formed in the mantle, this lighter, mobile melt rises, seeping and burning its way through the rocks of the crust. Many huge bubbles of magma do not break through to the surface, but stop rising within the crust, and slowly cool and harden into massive volumes of rock, called intrusions. The most familiar intrusions are of granite. However, where the magma is hot enough, or powerful enough to force a route all the way to the surface, we have a volcano.

Volcanoes are therefore simply the surface manifestation of magma escaping from the mantle. Everything about the volcano – how tall it can grow, how steep it is, whether it erupts quietly or explosively – is determined by the chemistry of the magma, and its journey to the surface.

A volcano grows in something like the same way as a fountain rises: the magmas rise because they have buoyancy relative to the rocks around them. Andesitic volcanoes can grow higher than basaltic volcanoes – as much as 7km (4 miles) above sea level in the Andes – because andesitic magmas are less dense.

Large volcanoes are an indication that the magma is taking the same route to the surface again and again. The existence of a volcano simply gets in the way of the dispersal of the magma out of the ground. Like a fountain in a deep freeze, the gradual build-up of solid material blocks the passage of the liquid, making it more difficult to escape. Unlike fountains, magma often seems to arrive from the mantle in batches, great bubbles consisting of billions of tons of molten rock. Therefore each new batch may find it more difficult to escape through the great solid cap of volcano. The pressure builds up until eventually something has to give way.

The least explosive volcanoes are those in which there is so much magma pouring up from the mantle that the volcano never completely "freezes" through. Volcanoes like Kilauea, on the largest island of the Hawaiian chain, and Mt Etna on Sicily, are

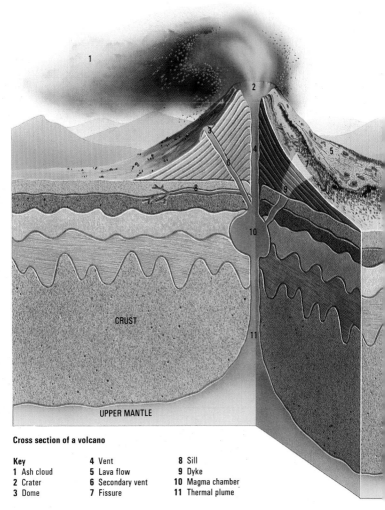

Cross section of a volcano

Key	4 Vent	8 Sill
1 Ash cloud	5 Lava flow	9 Dyke
2 Crater	6 Secondary vent	10 Magma chamber
3 Dome	7 Fissure	11 Thermal plume

really great balloons of magma with an outer shell of cold rock. The volcano periodically bleeds from one wound or another.

For many years the seismic observatory near Catania in Sicily was dogged by problems of noise that obscured the recording of distant earthquakes. There seemed no obvious source for this nearby, until finally a seismologist realized that the noise was the volcano itself, perpetually roaring and humming. The sound was actually coming from pipes within the volcano, along which magma was pouring, making noises like those produced as air moves through an organ pipe. Listening to Mt Etna's singing has shown scientists where the magma is moving, and where the next magma bleeding is likely to occur.

Mt Etna is a well organized volcano – the gas from the magma is released at the main crater, while the magma itself, free from gas, emerges out of a break in the flanks of the volcano. Hawaiian volcanoes erupt basaltic magmas which are fairly rich in gas, but the magma is very fluid, and as it pours out of a fissure, the gas escapes in a great fountain at the top end of the hole. Mt Kilauea

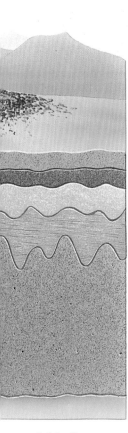

A magma fountain about 1500ft high (above), formed at the top end of a fissure eruption on Kilauea Iki, in 1959.

Magma pouring from the fissure forms a red-hot river that may flow all the way to the sea. The whole of Hawaii is built up of such flows.

and Mt Etna are volcanoes that erupt frequently, and provide relatively safe spectacles for observation.

Lava flows and ash clouds

It is hard to appreciate how rapidly the landscape of the magma-filled volcanoes, such as Etna or Kilauea, actually changes. On the summit of Etna you can climb to the crater one year and return ten years later to find the whole surroundings unfamiliar. In 1970 a small hole, or fumarole formed, through which gas was discharging. By 1982 it had widened to 200m (650ft) across – as large as the main crater.

For such volcanoes, the most frightening type of eruption can occur when the magma, instead of issuing from near the summit of the volcano, pours out from an opening near its base. The material may then be forced out under the full weight of the magma in the reservoir above the opening. Such an eruption took place on January 10 1977, when the great volcanic pile of Nyiragongo on the border of Zaïre and Rwanda, in central Africa, simply split

The tortured, sulfur-coated landscape (left and below) inside the crater of the volcano, Nyiragongo, Zaire. In 1977, the lava lake that had seethed and bubbled at the base of the crater for several decades suddenly emptied when the side of the volcano split open and a 60mph magma wave poured over the fertile mountain villages.

open like a ripe melon, along a crack 20km (12 miles) long. The volcano, 3,470m (11,000ft) high, contained a huge reservoir of magma that filled the base of the great crater, where it had seethed and bubbled for 50 years. The lowest point along the crack was 1,800m (6,000ft) below the lava lake and, just as if a great dam had burst at its base, the magma interconnections released molten rock to flood out of the fissures and pour across the land at speeds up to 60mph. The eruption overwhelmed more than 1,000 people living on the fertile flanks of the great mountain.

In general, however, it is very rare for people to be killed by lava flows, because normally the front of the magma stream, which is a chaotic mixture of partly solidified fragments of lava, travels at speeds slow enough to walk away from.

Magma by itself may not normally be a great threat to human life, but many volcanoes have other more terrible weapons to direct at the surrounding countryside. A variety of these are provided by the gas dissolved within the magma. As the magma rises and the pressure decreases, this gas emerges from the magma

Glassy top of a thin flow of fluid pahoehoe lava, running down a road on the island of Hawaii (left) is a complete contrast to the massive slow-flowing, largely solid lava that gradually overwhelmed much of the town of Vestmannaeyjar (below), on the island of Heimeay, Iceland in an eruption from the volcano Helgafell in 1973.

A rare photograph of a glowing avalanche (or nuée ardente) (above) pouring down the flanks of the volcano Ngauruhoe, New Zealand. The avalanche is a ground surge of gas and ash, caused by the partial collapse of the thick, eruptive cloud that has poured upwards from the volcano. Ground surges like this are now recognized as relatively common in major eruptions. Their effects can be deadly for anyone or anything in their path.

Resurrected from the dead: Pompeii, (right) inundated by mud and ash after the notorious eruption of Mt Vesuvius in AD79, stands exposed to the elements once more. Excavations involved the removal of up to 25ft of volcanic debris.

and immediately requires an enormous amount of space. As it expands it may burst into the air in fountains of molten rock which diffuse into tiny droplets and harden into fine ash.

Sometimes the hot gas may also pour high into the sky, carrying particles of ash and dust into the upper atmosphere, and forming a characteristic cloud in the shape of a pine tree. Such eruptions are termed plinian, after the Roman statesman and natural historian Pliny, who saw the pine-tree similarity in the cloud that formed over Mt Vesuvius as it began the eruption that destroyed the great town of Pompeii. Pliny himself was killed in the eruption whilst assisting in the evacuation.

Alternatively, the gas and magma may pour out in the form of a froth, which then surges down the side of a volcano to form a red-hot glowing avalanche or *nuée ardente*. It was a nuée ardente, moving at hurricane speed, that wreaked such destruction at St. Pierre in 1902.

Much of the danger of volcanoes is simply caused by elevation, which lends speed to whatever mixture of gas and magma has burst out of the crater, and sends it pouring down the flanks of the mountain. The ash commonly becomes mixed with water from melting ice and snow, crater lakes or even heavy rain, to form terrible volcanic mudslides known by the Indonesian word *lahar*.

Even the gases may roll downhill, if heavy enough. In 1979, a group of villagers walking along a footpath on the side of a Java-nese volcano were taken unawares by an eruption of gas from a pit higher up the flanks of the mountain. The gas was rich in heavier-than-air carbon dioxide, and it poured down the slope, displacing the oxygen-filled air as if it were a flood of water several feet deep. One hundred and fifty people died of suffocation over a distance of 400m (1,300ft), their bodies lying one behind the other.

s of white-hot magma that rise beneath a
enormous amount of energy – energy that can
owly or quickly. A gas cylinder may be used to
keep a flame burning for a long time – to cook food or to heat a
room. But the same energy in the gas may also be released all at
once in a single large explosion.

To understand why some volcanic eruptions are very explosive
while others are comparatively calm, we would have to look at the
hidden interior of the volcano. Volcano interiors are filled with a
sort of natural plumbing of tubes and pipes that connect through
the crust to the upper mantle. As in all plumbing, things only start
to go wrong when the pipes become blocked; and the blocking, like
boiler scale or frozen water, is generally caused by the fluid
material itself – in this case the magma that may solidify or
become too sticky to flow easily. Pressure builds up, and something
eventually has to break. That breakage is finally the volcano itself
– the result of the breakage is a volcanic eruption.

A magma-gas explosion involves the sudden increase of volume
of gases under very high pressures. This increase in volume sets up
a shock wave through the air. Magma arrives at the surface from
deep in the earth where it was formed under very high pressures;
and as it travels toward the surface this pressure is released. Dissolved in the magma are gases. These gases are kept trapped in the
magma by the pressure, and as the pressure is released, the gases

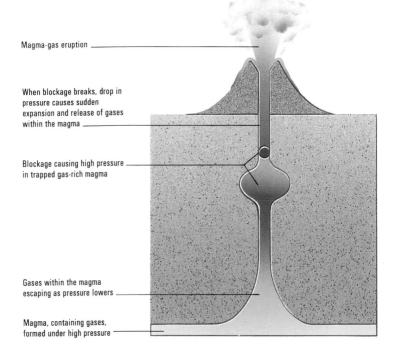

Magma-gas eruption

When blockage breaks, drop in
pressure causes sudden
expansion and release of gases
within the magma

Blockage causing high pressure
in trapped gas-rich magma

Gases within the magma
escaping as pressure lowers

Magma, containing gases,
formed under high pressure

escape. Take a bottle of champagne – uncork it slowly and the gases will gently fizz. Uncork it faster and the rapid release of gas will make the cork fly off and cause foaming champagne to pour from the bottle. The explosive power of the gas is dependent on how rapidly the pressure is released.

Therefore an explosive eruption requires magma that is rich in gas. Yet if it is too fluid it will readily escape to the surface. Therefore the most explosive eruptions involve a sticky magma full of gas. In the reservoir of magma under the volcano, the pressure may gradually build up, until eventually the weight may be slightly dislodged. A small drop in pressure causes a great release of gas – the sudden expansion can blow the top off a mountain.

Some of the stickiest gas-rich magmas are those which form above the subduction zones. It is therefore these that cause some of the most dangerous and explosive eruptions. Volcanoes such as Mt Pelée, Mt St Helens, and Krakatoa are all in this category. Others form a garland around the Pacific (the "ring of fire") with a side chain passing through Indonesia. There are also local arcs of volcanoes in the West Indies, South Sandwich Islands and through the Mediterranean.

The water-magma bomb

The principle of the steam engine is very simple. Steam is produced by boiling water and, as the steam occupies a volume more than 200 times that of the original water, this causes expansion

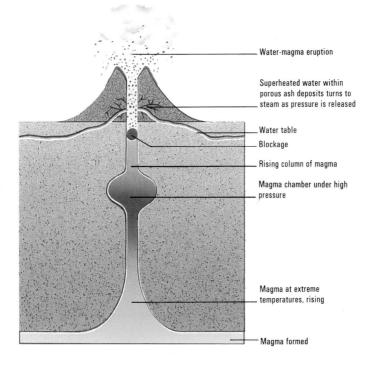

Water-magma eruption

Superheated water within porous ash deposits turns to steam as pressure is released

Water table

Blockage

Rising column of magma

Magma chamber under high pressure

Magma at extreme temperatures, rising

Magma formed

which can be used to push a piston. To turn this process into an explosion, the increase in volume has to be resisted. Leaving a sealed can full of water in a fire leads to just such an explosion.

The magma beneath a volcano is an enormous source of heat. If water comes into contact with the magma it will heat up, but under high pressures, hot water at temperatures far above boiling point may be prevented from changing to steam. Release that pressure and the water flashes to steam with an enormous increase in volume.

Hot water in the porous old ash deposits lying above the magma reservoir may eventually burst through the overburden. As the first crack appears, the pressure suddenly drops, turning all the water into steam and causing a large explosion. Such explosions are known as "phreatic" eruptions. They are often the first eruptions to occur as the volcano comes to life, and the magma is rising through the water-saturated rock.

However, far larger explosions may occur when the water comes into contact with the magma itself. As water expands into steam, it opens up new channels which can break through to the sea bed. Water breaks into the magma and turns to steam, forcing a larger crack down which still more water passes, all of it flashing to steam, and the crack gets larger and the amount of water passing in gets larger until the whole mass of magma and steam blows itself up. This is called a chain reaction – a sequence of small events quickly builds up to a terrible conclusion. To create such a magma bomb there has to be a large chamber of magma, and an effectively limitless supply of water – such as the sea.

At one o'clock in the afternoon of August 26 1883, the fuse had been lit on a magma bomb beneath the island of Krakatoa, located between Sumatra and Java, Indonesia. For three months the volcano had been rumbling and puffing. Suddenly, there occurred the first of a series of explosions of increasing intensity. After an hour the volcano built an ash cloud 25km (15 miles) high. The noise of the explosions "destroyed the eardrums" of half the crew of a British vessel located 40km (25 miles) away. Then, shortly after 10am the following morning, the island of Krakatoa largely blew itself out of existence: the magma chamber beneath the volcano exploded, sending ash and gas surging almost to the outer limits of the atmosphere 80km (50 miles) above the sea. What was left of the original volcano sank into the hole that had formerly been the magma chamber, and as the sea burst into the chasm that had formed, a huge wave spread out from the disturbance – a tsunami which burst over all the low-lying regions of Sumatra and Java, close to the straits, reaching elevations up to 30m (100ft) above normal sea level. The explosion was almost certainly the work of the magma-water chain reaction. A few fragments of islands now define the edge of the hole, or caldera.

The Krakatoa magma bomb, seen just before the entire island blew up in 1883 (opposite above). More than 36,000 people were killed in the eruption and ensuing tsunami, one of the worst ever known. But the event was studied and mapped in every detail (opposite below), providing data that will one day be of great use.

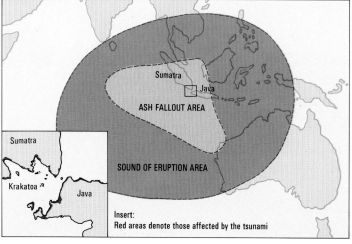

Insert:
Red areas denote those affected by the tsunami

Historic eruptions

It is relatively simple to identify volcanoes that are non-explosive, and also those more likely to erupt explosively. But in the majority of cases, even these "dangerous" volcanoes are unlikely to be very explosive. This is because it is easier for nature to create a "poor" explosion – one in which the energy release is not concentrated in a single instant – than an explosion capable of destroying a large island, like that at Krakatoa. Scientists estimate that the eruption of Krakatoa in 1883 released a quantity of energy similar to that of an entirely "peaceful" eruption of magma from the Hawaiian volcano of Mauna Loa in 1950, in which all the energy was released slowly in the form of heat. Of all eruptions, less than one in a hundred is explosive. Such rapid and catastrophic phases of eruption are termed "paroxysms".

Even Krakatoa was not the largest eruption of the past two centuries. That honor belongs to the volcano Tambora, on the island of Sumbawa, Indonesia, which exploded between April 5 and 10, 1815. Four thousand meters (13,000ft) high, the volcano lost 1,000m (3,500ft) in elevation as more than 150 cu km (40 cu miles) of debris was thrown into the sky. All that remains now is a caldera, measuring 6km × 5km (4 × 3 miles) and 1,300m (4,000ft) deep. The eruption deposited ash over a radius of more than 620 miles.

Another major eruption took place on June 6 1912 at Mt

Katmai, at the eastern end of the Alaskan peninsula. Mt Katmai was originally more than 7,500ft high before the eruption blew out the interior of the volcano, leaving the summit to collapse into a caldera 5km (3 miles) across and more than 1,000m (3,500ft) deep. The explosion was heard up to 750 miles away, and the ash from the eruption was deposited up to a distance of 950 miles. More than 60 miles from the volcano, at the village of Kodiak, the ash caused a darkness that lasted 60 hours and was "so thick it was impossible to see a lantern at arm's length."

However, the most remarkable feature of the event was a great fissure eruption of magma froth and ash. This poured into a wooded valley located to the northwest of the volcano, flowing over 12 miles and filling the terrain to a thickness estimated at 250m (800ft) with fragments of magma and ash so hot that, at depth, they had fused into a glassy rock known as *ignimbrite*. The volume of material erupted into this valley was estimated at 11 cu km (3 cu miles). For many years after the eruption, the water and vegetation beneath the ashes continued to give off steam, and became known as the "valley of ten thousand smokes."

The Katmai eruption is the only historical eruption known to have produced the rock ignimbrite. The process probably requires a very rapid eruption of enormous quantities of magma froth, so that the whole deposit is sufficiently hot and thick for all the separate fragments to be welded together.

The greatest known eruption in history: the volcano Tambora (left) created a caldera 7km (4 miles) in diameter in 1815, as shown in this Landsat image of Sumbawa Island, Indonesia.

A Krakatoa of the past (above). A volcanic plug has grown up in the middle of a sea-flooded caldera, which is now a perfect natural harbor at Rabaul, Papua New Guinea in the western Pacific ocean.

The largest known eruption in the past 2,000 years probably occurred in the Taupo volcanic center, in New Zealand's North Island. Sometime around AD150 there was an eruption that, in eight individual spasms, ejected over 25 cu km (6 cu miles) of ignimbrite debris over almost all of the North Island, covering about 52,000 sq km (20,000 sq miles) of the land area with more than 100mm (4in) of volcanic deposits – sufficient to kill almost all the vegetation. The material erupted was a magma froth that cooled to form ignimbrite, pouring out of the volcano at a speed sufficient to climb ridges 1,000m (3,500ft) higher than the crater out of which it had spewed. Ten similar cataclysmic eruptions are known from Taupo in the past million years. This at least suggests that the next one may be some way in the future.

Large earthquakes seem to be at least ten times more common than large volcanic eruptions. We have good reason to believe that the largest known fault movements – such as those that caused the Chilean earthquake of 1960 and the Alaskan earthquake of 1964, are unlikely ever to be far exceeded. To put it another way, in any century we are likely to have earthquakes at the top end of the scale. However, we know that much bigger volcanic eruptions

1,800 years ago an enormous eruption bursting out from Lake Taupo volcanic center in North Island, New Zealand (left) engulfed almost the whole island (52,000 sq km/ 20,000 sq miles) in magma froth and ash. The Taupo area has a long history – over the last million years – of such eruptions.

Crater Lake, Oregon (below), was formed 7,000 years ago, when former Mt Mazama blew itself to destruction, the remains of the mountain collapsing into the empty magma chamber, 600m (2,000ft) deep and 10km (6 miles) wide. A new ''Mt Mazama'', the cone of Wizard Island, has begun to form inside the caldera.

have occurred in the distant past than have been observed in the historical period: it may take ten thousand years of monitoring before we could be fairly certain of recording the largest eruptions that take place.

In prehistory, the eruption that blew the top off Mt Mazama in southern Oregon removed at least 3,500ft of the mountain and its thick glaciers, which were formerly up to 1,000ft thick and 12 miles long. The remaining caldera, Crater Lake, is 10km (6 miles) in diameter and 600m (2,000ft) deep. The eruption caused a succession of nuées ardentes to spread right over the plains up to 30 or 40 miles away.

Beyond Tambora, beyond Crater Lake, beyond Taupo, there are still more massive and shadowy eruptions. Among the contenders for the largest known must be a caldera measuring 30km by 90km (20 miles by 60 miles) in Sumatra, which was formed 20,000 years ago in an eruption so vast that it deposited layers of volcanic debris over 25,000 sq km (10,000 sq miles), with thicknesses up to 300m (1,000ft). Twenty thousand years is an instant in geological time. When and where will the next giant eruption take place?

The effects of volcanoes

Volcanoes are not usually perceived as a direct threat. But you do not have to have a volcano on your doorstep to suffer its effects.

At the end of June, 1982, a British Airways Boeing 747 was flying with 240 passengers on a scheduled flight from Singapore to Australia, at a height of 37,000ft. Across the airplane's flight path the crew observed a strange dark cloud. The airplane entered the cloud, and soon afterwards its engines cut out one by one, to be replaced by a terrifying silence. The plane went into a controlled glide as the pilot desperately tried to restart the engines. The glide lasted 16 minutes as the aircraft lost 24,500ft by which time many of the passengers had resigned themselves to certain death. Eventually, at the last possible moment, the pilot managed to set the turbines spinning and restarted three of the engines – enough to make an emergency landing at Jakarta.

Unknowingly, the passengers of the British Airways flight had almost become victims of a volcanic eruption. For two months the Indonesian volcano Galunggung had been erupting intermittently, and now a vigorous new phase had sent large quantities of

dust into the upper atmosphere. The aircraft had been flying on its normal route, 90 miles from the volcano; but the lessons of how far these volcanic dust clouds drift was not immediately learnt. Two weeks later, a Singapore Airlines 747 on the same route stalled three engines in another ash plume from the same volcano; after falling 8,000ft, the pilot managed to restart one engine and landed safely in Jakarta. Jet engines were not designed to be operated at high speeds in a dust storm – the dust abrades the turbines and clogs the fuel lines.

Dust in the atmosphere

In the summer of 1816, New England farmers found that the crops they had planted grew very slowly, and much of the fruit failed to ripen. The weather was unseasonably cold, with widespread snow between June 6 and June 11, and frosts in each of the summer months. The situation was the same on the other side of the Atlantic, particularly in Britain and Scandinavia. From May to October there was almost continuous rain, the temperature in

The Plinian clouds of ash and gas over the volcano of Galunggung, Indonesia (above and left), from the eruption of June 1982. The ash brought traffic to a halt in distant towns, and – closer to the volcano – all but overwhelmed villages. A total of 75,000 people were evacuated from the area. 93 miles from the volcano, dust choked the engines of two airplanes, narrowly avoiding major disasters.

London was 3–6°F (2–3°C) below normal, and the poor harvests in Ireland and Wales led to severe food shortages. The year of 1816 was labelled the "year without a summer."

In the middle of the previous year, 1815, a volcano located on the other side of the world from New England and Europe, Tambora on Sumbawa, Indonesia, produced the largest eruption of the past two centuries. The quantities of fine ash that had been blown into the upper atmosphere were so great that the solar heat reaching the Earth's surface may have declined by as much as one-fifth. In 1816 there were no accurate measurements of the level of the sun's radiation, but from the late 19th century, when careful measurements were being taken, it was possible to show that for the two years after the eruption of Krakatoa in 1883, and also for the two years after the eruption of Mount Katmai (in Alaska in 1912), the level of solar radiation had been more than 10 percent below average. Most recently the eruption of El Chichón in Mexico, in 1982, shot great volumes of dust, as if from a cannon, straight into the upper atmosphere. So the consequences of a major eruption may be felt worldwide.

The upper atmosphere is very sensitive to dust. It has been calculated that a reduction in solar radiation by 20 percent would require only 1/400 of a cubic kilometer (1/1600 of a cubic mile) of very fine-grained dust in the upper atmosphere. If this amount was continually resupplied to the atmosphere every two years, the average temperature of the planet would decrease by about 10°F (5.6°C). Such a decline in temperatures would cause extraordinary changes in climate, producing a great increase in the permanent snow cover, and could even be a factor in triggering off a new

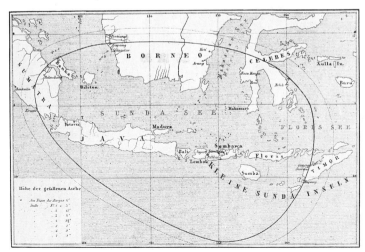

Ashfall from the 1815 Tambora eruption on the island of Sumbawa, observed and mapped by Swiss scientist Heinrich Zollinger in 1847. The dotted line shows estimated total extent of ashfall.

Debris from the eruption, carried up into the stratosphere, reflected back sunlight and may have played a part in the bad harvests recorded at that time.

ice age. The studies of volcanic dust have also shown how man could all too easily produce the effects of volcanoes. In a nuclear war the transport of dust into the upper atmosphere would lower the levels of solar radiation. Nuclear explosions, like many volcanic eruptions, could create an effect far more severe than that known after the single volcanic eruption at Tambora.

Sleeping volcanoes

Do you know where your nearest volcano is? You may have been told where the nearest "active" volcano is located; but the terms "active," "dormant" and "extinct," which were formerly used for volcanoes, have frequently had to be reconsidered. Every year or so a volcano that was "extinct" has to be transferred to the active list. The problem is simply one of time scale. "Active" denotes a volcano that has erupted when there were people present and able to make written records of the eruption. For most regions of the globe, this may only mean within the past two centuries. Yet, just as with earthquakes, the volcano cycle (the time between one eruption and the next) may be as much as thousands, or even tens of thousands of years. Therefore the categories we should use are "active," "probably extinct," and "unproven." Many volcanoes lie in this last category: we never know when they may wish to come out of retirement.

Volcanoes are unlike earthquakes, you might think, at least in having visible warnings. A volcanic mountain is like a red flag on a shooting range, reminding us that this area is potentially dangerous. Yet volcanoes do not always look like great conical mountains. There are numerous beautiful lakes, surrounded by

Deceptively calm, the crater lake of Haleakala, Hawaii, the world's largest "dormant" volcano. As with earthquakes, volcanic eruptions follow a cycle that may allow tens, hundreds or thousands of years to elapse between one disturbance and the next. Many apparently extinct volcanoes may simply be passing through a quiescent stage.

Eroded volcanic craters on the Galapagos Islands, providing rich and varied landscapes and exotic wildlife habitats. As Charles Darwin discovered, the creation of new volcanic islands allows isolated experiments in species evolution.

forested hills and picturesque villages – in Guatemala, in Italy, in Indonesia and in New Zealand – that are really no more than volcanic craters, produced by cataclysmic eruptions which destroyed any pretence of a conical mountain. Some day, one or other of these beautiful lakes will begin to seethe and boil as a new volcano emerges from the depths.

Out at sea there are many small groups of steep-sided islands located in a ring of fragments, and along the coastline there are sections that define an almost perfect arc of a circle – these are no more than the remains of volcanic craters. After only a few

The inhabitants of this pretty lake-side village in West Germany may not realize that they are living on the brink of a volcanic crater that in the not-too-distant past was erupting fire and stones across the surrounding fertile countryside.

hundred years, a lot of small volcanoes and craters have become very well disguised – the rich soils create a camouflage of dense and luxuriant vegetation.

Whether these craters are sleeping or dead, we often cannot tell. While Europeans know all about volcanoes in Italy, few realize that in the centre of France there are a series of volcanoes which last erupted a few thousand years ago, and will almost certainly erupt again. Only 30 miles to the south of Cologne, in the industrial heartland of Western Europe, there are volcanic craters which last erupted explosively only 11,000 years ago, depositing a series of ash layers that can be traced from Italy to Finland. How much havoc would a renewed eruption in Germany play with air-flights, agriculture, commerce?

Inside the volcano

As we have seen, some of the fiercest eruptions, as at Krakatoa and Santorini, occur when volcanoes are located close to sea level and a great battle takes place between red-hot magma and the water. One of the strangest locations for any town in the world must be that of Pozzuoli, Italy, which is effectively built within the crater of an active volcano. This crater is extremely large – so large in fact that at first sight it might pass unnoticed. It was formed in a giant explosive eruption 34,000 years ago, a mere yesterday in geological time, in which 250,000 million tons of debris were erupted over an area of almost one million square miles.

The collapsed caldera that resulted from this eruption is 7-9 miles wide, and half of it is underwater at the western end of the

Bay of Naples. The landward crater is known as the Campi Flegrei (Phlegraean Fields), a region of volcanic craters, fumaroles and hot springs. Beneath the crater and the region of the Phlegraean Fields, there lies a large magma chamber that is gradually cooling, contracting and solidifying. Four thousand years ago, a crater was formed in the area, at a place called Solfatara, which still remains the site of continuous fumarole activity; this is where tourists can have rocks, crockery or any solid object sulfur-coated in a natural steam jet.

The last outburst from the Phlegraean Fields came in 1538, when a new volcanic cone was formed in the middle of a crater lake just inland from Pozzuoli, called Monte Nuovo. As the underlying magma chamber cools, the eruptions have retreated inward towards the center – which lies right under the town of Pozzuoli.

This town was once a thriving Roman port, across the bay from Pompeii. In the 1820s a visiting English geologist came across one of its Roman monuments, an ancient temple. Although it was now surrounded by fields, he realized that marine borings at a height of more than ten feet indicated that since its construction the temple must have been for a dip in the Mediterranean before it re-emerged onto dry land. Vertical movements began to be monitored in 1819, and from then until 1968 the area continued to sink, leading to a subsidence of around 8ft at an average rate of half an inch per year. Around 1969 the movement changed direction: the town of Pozzuoli began to rise in two rapid pulses, being elevated by 1.7m (5.5ft) between 1970 and 1972, and by 1.8m (6ft) between 1983 and 1985. Between these two pulses the town sank

The town of Pozzuoli, Italy had risen half a meter between 1982 (left) and 1984 (right), elevated by movements in an underlying magma chamber. The columns of the Roman Temple of Serapis are the town's dipstick – marine borings 3m (10ft) up, record a period of submergence.

back 20cm (8in). While the first uplift passed without incident, the second was accompanied by damaging earthquakes, suggesting that the brittle crust overlying the magma chamber, thought to lie at a depth of about 5km (3 miles), was becoming fractured. These fractures are most likely associated with rising magma.

As a result of the earthquakes, over half of the 72,000 people of Pozzuoli were evacuated and almost 8,000 homes may have to be demolished. The fishing fleet has had to move because the harbor is now too shallow.

This recent upwelling will probably lead to some kind of eruption – but when? Between 1501-3, the coast of Pozzuoli rose out of the sea in the same fashion, and less than 40 years later there was an eruption in a lake about two miles away that produced a new volcanic cone (called Monte Nuovo) more than 300ft high. Will the next eruption produce another small cone, like Monte Nuovo, or could it perhaps produce a magma-water eruption like that at Krakatoa? Only time will tell.

Monte Nuovo surprised and entertained the citizens around Naples – to them a new mountain had been born, but we now recognize that it simply emerged from a lake that was itself the site of an earlier crater. Like trees, new volcanoes grow as shoots on the sites of their fallen parents. Yet even the largest of volcanoes had to begin some time. There is always the nightmare that a volcano could suddenly start to form where there was none before.

A volcano is born

In June 1759, the people of the village of Hacienda de Jorullo, located about 200 miles to the west of Mexico City, began to hear underground rumblings. These became stronger and stronger, shaking the ground and shattering the chapel. A priest was instructed to go to Jorullo, and on September 21 he began a nine-day Mass, continually interrupted by earthquakes and explosions. At 3am on September 29, at the base of a nearby gully, a great cloud of steam arose, followed by "cinders, fire and thunder." Over the next few years, the volcano rose 1,500ft above the plain. Pouring out lava and ash, it completely overwhelmed a number of villages and laid waste the surrounding countryside.

Almost 200 years later, and 90 miles to the northwest of Jorullo, on a small piece of land belonging to a certain Dionisio Pulido, there was a hollow in the rock where local children used to play. One old lady remembered that 50 years earlier she had hidden in the pit and had heard sounds coming from underground; the rocks had also been strangely warm. Then, on February 5 1943, the villagers of Paricutin began to feel small earthquakes, and the tremors grew stronger and more frequent every day. On February 20, Dionisio left as usual to tend his fields. In the late afternoon he saw a crack appear in the ground passing through the hole. With a sound of thunder, and a shudder of the earth, the ground bulged up and smoke poured out of the crack, followed by sparks that set some nearby trees alight.

Dionisio had just witnessed the birth of a volcano. An hour later some curious villagers gathered to see red-hot rock emerge from a hole at the end of the crack, a hole which grew bigger in front of them. At midnight, the hole sent incandescent lava bombs up into the sky, and lightning played around the ash cloud. Dionisio returned to his fields at 8am to find that a cone 35ft high had grown in his cornfield. The activity was speeding up – by midday the cone was 100-160ft high, and by nightfall lava had begun to pour out slowly from the base of the cone. The following day, Dionisio had no farm. After a week the volcano had grown to a height of 140m (460ft), and there was a continuous thundering roar as fragments of magma were thrown more than half a mile into the air. The noise could be heard 200 miles away. After a month, a 20,000ft-high column of ash and dust had formed over the volcano, falling on all the area around. During the next year great lava fountains, explosions and ash showers occurred as the volcano grew to 1,000ft, and by the time activity finally ceased in 1952, the summit towered 1,350ft above Dionisio's cornfield.

There are hundreds of similar cones in this region of Mexico – formed in single eruptions and never reused. Might a volcano begin to erupt in your back garden overnight? In some volcanic regions this is always a possibility. There have also been claims in certain parts of the world that magma is at this moment slowly ascending towards the surface, one day to create a new volcano in places as diverse as Belgium and Japan.

Offshore, new volcanoes like the Island of Surtsey to the south of Iceland, born in 1963, are more common. Yet many new small volcanic islands are soon overwhelmed by the sea. Others grow like oak trees from acorns – even the great island of Hawaii was once no more than a single volcanic cone a few yards high, protruding from the Pacific swell.

Half-buried by advancing lava flow from Paracutin volcano, a church tower stands as the last visible landmark of San Juan Parangaricutiro village. In its 9 active years, the volcano ejected an estimated 3.6 billion tons of material.

Violent explosions from a mysterious submarine source occurred just off the coast of Iceland in November 1963. The activity proved to be volcanic, and marked the birth of Surtsey, a brand new island.

Volcanic mudslides

Unlike earthquakes, you cannot build a house that can withstand many of the weapons of a major volcanic eruption. In such an event, the only hazard a house is likely to survive is ash fall; but even so, a surprising amount of danger threatens houses near a volcano after a long unexplosive eruption, simply from the weight of ash piled on roofs.

The most easily predicted consequence of an eruption is that of volcanic mudslides – the lahars. If there is an ice cap or crater lake on the volcano, or if the region is subject to torrential rains, then lahars are highly probable after a sudden eruption. Lahars are no more than great thick muddy floods that follow the same course as the streams. It is therefore sensible to build houses away from the low-lying valleys. The lahars at the Nevado del Ruiz volcano in Columbia (1985) were predicted precisely because they had happened before. It had been recognized that any significant eruption was likely to melt the ice cap and send lahars pulsing down the Lagunillas River into the town of Armero, because identical mudflows had occurred in the past.

Armero was just unlucky. There are millions of people around the globe living in the paths of future volcanic mudslides. One does not need to go to the developing world to find dangerously sited towns like Armero. In Washington State, USA, there are glaciers

on Mount Rainier, nearly 15,000ft high and overlooking Seattle, that in the event of an eruption are certain to melt. What has happened in the past? Long before settlers moved into the region, there had been many mudflows down the valleys leading to Puget Sound; 5,000 years ago one lahar traveled 40 miles, burying what are now thriving towns and suburbs under many tens of feet of mud and boulders.

Crater lakes can sometimes present a hazard – at the Kelut volcano in Eastern Java, Indonesia, mud flows caused by eruptions of the crater lake bursting down the fertile flanks of the mountain have claimed thousands of lives. In 1919, Dutch engineers dug tunnels through the crater, lowering the water level by more than 160ft, and reducing the lake's volume by 95 percent. However, a new eruption in 1951 destroyed the tunnel intakes, and deepened the crater. Even after the tunnel had been repaired, in 1966 a new eruption killed hundreds of people in mudslides. In 1967 a new low tunnel was completed in an attempt to remove the hazard.

Crater lakes may burst some considerable time after an eruption. The dams holding up the lakes may be very fragile. In 1953, eight years after an eruption, the lake on the volcano of Ruapehu, in North Island, New Zealand, burst through a wall of ash and ice, sending a massive flood down the Whangaehu River, carrying

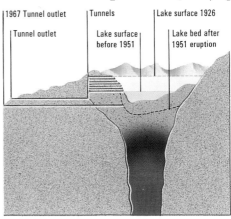

1967 Tunnel outlet | Tunnels | Lake surface 1926

Tunnel outlet | Lake surface before 1951 | Lake bed after 1951 eruption

Torrential mudflows caused by the Nevada del Ruiz eruption of 1985 completely buried the town of Armero, Colombia. Evacuation orders were issued, but too late for most of the 23,000 inhabitants, who were interred in their homes by an avalanche of mud up to 12ft deep.

A specially designed tunnel system at Kelut volcano, Java, keeps the crater lake at a safe, low level, preventing floods and mudflows.

trees, rocks and icebergs. It was 8pm on Christmas Eve, and a crowded express train from Wellington to Auckland was advancing toward the river when the wall of water hit the railroad bridge, destroying it and sending the train plunging into the flooded ravine, with the loss of 151 lives.

Death and destruction

For the more explosive hazards, such as nuées ardentes, the path the avalanche follows may be hard to predict. Such avalanches have been known to travel uphill over low ridges and to enter valleys which do not lead directly from the volcano. Lateral eruptions, such as those emerging from Mt St Helens in 1982, can destroy everything in their path, 12 miles from the volcano. If there had been towns to the north of Mt St Helens, these would have been destroyed as effectively as the town of St Pierre was destroyed by the 1902 eruption of Mt Pelée. In such circumstances, the only protection is evacuation.

In the largest known eruptions, most deaths have come not from the direct effects of the products of the volcano, but second-hand. In the 1883 eruption of Krakatoa, almost all the deaths were caused not by the explosion but by the tsunami that claimed 36,000 lives in the coastal towns and villages. In the great fissure eruptions in Iceland in 1783, enormous quantities of gas emerged

Bursting through a thin wall of ice and ash, the crater lake of Ruapehu volcano, New Zealand, overwhelmed a crowded train on December 24 1953. This national catastrophe occurred eight years after the original eruption.

with the vast basaltic lava flows, covering the whole country with a poison fog that killed all vegetation. Fifty percent of the horses, 80 percent of the sheep and 10 percent of the human population died from disease and starvation, and the whole agricultural economy of the island came to a halt. In the Tambora eruption of 1815, 10,000 people were killed in the eruption, but more than 80,000 later died from hunger and disease as the ash fall killed off the vegetation across Sumbawa and the neighboring islands.

Such giant eruptions have not yet occurred in the 20th century in a highly populated region. Tsunami hazard from a nearby volcanic cataclysm may be very hard to anticipate – and while starvation can now be avoided, the economic cost of the total disruption of a large community would today be measured in terms of billions of dollars. As with earthquakes, attention must shift onto eruption prediction.

In theory, eruption prediction is relatively simple. There are many indicators to show that a mountain is reawakening. Earthquakes often occur as the magma rises; the mountain may begin to heat up and to swell. Gases emitted by the magma will tend to emerge ahead of it, and measurement of such gases as sulfur dioxide are frequently used to show that new magma is close to the surface. In 1980, volcanologists had the opportunity to test out all they had learnt on a volcano in the Western United States.

The story of Mt St Helens

The beautiful volcanic peak of Mt St Helens in the Cascade Range of Western USA, dormant for over a century, had excited much admiration but little concern previous to the cataclysm of May 1980. Its true identity, however, was to become all too obvious in the course of that year.

On March 27, the volcano began to stir from its long slumber with a number of small earthquakes beneath the mountain. Then a new crater started to open in the ice and snow at the summit, and a series of small "phreatic" eruptions began, caused by heating of the water in the volcano, with an outburst of old ash. There was very little sulfur dioxide in the gases being released, and therefore little thought was given to the possibility of a new magmatic outburst. However, the area around the volcano was restricted in the recognition of the possible hazard from ice avalanches and mudflows.

The eruptions decreased through April and May, but the whole northern part of the mountain above the zone of earthquakes, about 2km (just over a mile) in diameter, was found to be bulging outward at about 1.5m (5ft) each day. There was still no increase in sulfur dioxide, but the bulge, which now protruded 150m (500ft), was clearly caused by the rise of a column of magma.

Mt St Helens: before, during, after. Previous to the eruption of May 1980 (top), Mt St Helens was the most beautiful peak of the Pacific coast's Cascade Range. Then, on May 18 1980, it literally blew its top (left). An earthquake shook loose the unstable bulge that had formed above the magma chamber, and the pressure release induced an explosion that ripped sideways through the north face of the mountain. A second explosion went straight upwards. Four years later (above), the landscape of St Helens is still desolate.

However, the possibility that the bulge might turn into a landslide had been considered.

Then on the bright sunny morning of Sunday May 18, and without any warning whatsoever, a big earthquake occurred at the volcano. This displaced the whole north face of the mountain, turning it into an enormous avalanche of ice, rock and mud. The sudden pressure release caused the hot water-saturated rock and the magma beneath it to expel a lateral blast of ash and hot gas at speeds faster than a hurricane, felling all the trees in its path.

Meanwhile a cloud of gas and ash also shot up vertically, forming a Plinian eruption up to 20km (12 miles) high. The eruption lasted for about 9 hours and by its end, the mountain top had vanished, leaving in its place a crater 1.5km (1 mile) across and 1km (just over half a mile) deep. In less than a day the volcano had changed from a beautiful snow-capped mountain to a lifeless wasteland. The maps would have to be redrawn – the volcano had lost 400m (1,300ft) in elevation.

A good number of lessons were learnt at Mt St Helens. While the reawakening of the volcano had been closely monitored, the nature of the eruption had not been predicted. This was not scientific negligence. The volcano had been much more rotten that had been anticipated, and lateral blasts had not occurred in the volcano's past.

The difficulties of prediction

Only three out of one hundred eruptions are likely to cause great danger to people living and working around the volcano. The eruption of Mt St Helens was one of that dangerous minority. El Chichón in Mexico was another such eruption. Could it have been predicted? We will never know – it was in a remote area, and although there had been local tremors, the volcano was not being closely monitored when it blew up on March 28 1982.

In 1976, on the island of Guadeloupe, there was a series of local tremors that suggested that the volcano of Soufrière was coming back to life. Was the forthcoming eruption going to be a repeat of the 1902 Mt Pelée eruption, which destroyed the town of St. Pierre, on nearby Martinique? The volcano began a series of small outbursts, and the authorities were encouraged to evacuate 75,000 of the inhabitants closest to the volcano.

Fifteen minor eruptions occurred between July 1976 and March 1977, all of them apparently "phreatic," caused by the reaction of ground-water with the volcano's heat, but there was no evidence of new magma arriving at the surface. The evacuation lasted for about four months. The loss of jobs and crops, and the complete disruption of the local economy, was estimated to have cost up to $500 million. The evacuation had been unnecessary.

As with the prediction of earthquakes, early euphoria about eruptions whose behavior was fairly well estimated has since been dispelled by the experience of subsequent eruptions, whose nature was not anticipated. Yet every volcanic eruption provides important lessons, and the ones that seem most unpredictable provide the most important lessons of all. Even before earthquake

The eruption that didn't happen.
Mt Soufriere, Guadeloupe, in 1976
threatened an eruption on the scale of the

1902 Mt Pelée disaster. An evacuation
involving 70,000 people was organized, but
the eruption never occurred.

predictors had to grapple with the social implications of their science, the volcanologists learned the hard way – that erring on the side of caution, encouraging an evacuation when the volcano does not explode, wins you no friends. That loss of confidence among volcanologists regarding the importance of their opinions might even have contributed to the situation in Colombia in 1985 when there was a hesitancy to effect an evacuation in time.

The stark truth of the unpredictability of certain volcanoes is to be found from the way in which volcanologists themselves have sometimes lost their lives in unforeseen eruptions. On September 17 1952, a Japanese fishing boat noticed a submarine eruption 400km (250 miles) south of Tokyo. At first, a small island appeared, but this was soon destroyed in a series of explosions. Two research ships sailed to investigate the volcano – the first to arrive, the *Sinyo-maru*, observed a series of violent explosions from a distance. The second, the *Kaiyo-maru*, with a crew of 22, plus 7 scientists, was sailing directly over the underwater vent when an eruption took place. The boat was destroyed and there were no survivors. The volcanologist David Johnston was himself killed while observing the unexpected violence of the Mt St Helens eruption.

Volcanic products as fertilizers

Having seen the number of hazards that volcanoes present – lava flows, ash falls, tsunamis, pyroclastic flows – it may seem hard to comprehend why people wish to live near them. Yet, while the hazards are multifarious, they are generally, except for some of the Indonesian volcanoes, relatively rare – and the benefits can be large. In many areas of modern life, we enjoy certain benefits while recognizing that certain risks may be attached to them; from skiing, to flying in an airplane, to living next door to a petro-chemical refinery. Living near a volcano has always represented a similar mixture of risks and benefits.

Volcanoes are places where new rock is created from the fountains of magma that rise up from the mantle. Just as men have always built their settlements around natural springs where fresh water emerges from the ground, so volcanoes, as natural springs of new rock, have attracted men to build towns and villages close to this great resource.

New fresh rock has many advantages. It is full of minerals formed at high temperatures, which quickly break down when attacked by water to release their elements, providing essential nutrients for plants. In the aftermath of a major eruption of volcanic ash, farmers (at a distance) often enjoy greatly improved harvests.

After an eruption from Soufrière, St Vincent, in May 1812, the ash known as "May dust" was treasured, and every pile of it was used. In the immediate aftermath of the eruption there was a fear of starvation, but the crops that had been planted grew so fast, and produced such good yields, that within a few months there was an excess of food. In areas some distance from the ash eruptions of Vesuvius, Iceland and Paracutín, where there was a thin fall of only a few inches of ash, the crops are generally reported to have improved. The fall of ash on the island of Kodiak, after the 1912 Katmai (Alaska) outburst, created such luxuriant grass and such bountiful berries that it was considered "the best thing that ever happened to Kodiak." It is even claimed that some of the tribes from the Papua New Guinea Highlands perform dances to bring fresh ash falls.

It is not just farmers who benefit from the magma springs. Scarce mineral elements emerge from the mantle into the crust through volcanic action, elements like copper, gold, lead, platinum, chromium, manganese, aluminum – the very materials of technology. Most of these elements are in the magma in very low concentrations, and it would be uneconomic to attempt to extract gold or copper from simple lava flows. But volcanoes are also capable of doing their own mineral concentration. For they do not just bring the fresh rock to the surface; volcanoes act like enormously complicated factories and refineries, stuffed with intricate networks of pipes and fissures, filled with water, steam, gas and magma, and all of it changing through time as eruptions come and go. This great industrial complex which lies beneath the volcano is powered by the enormous centralized heat source provided by the magma itself.

Subterranean natural refineries
In places where these hot-water pipes emerge at the surface, there are hot springs. Frequently, these hot springs supply thick deposits of minerals around their mouths in extraordinary natural sculptures, simultaneously carved by and crystallized from the water.

As the pressure increases down the pipe, so too does the temperature at which water can remain without boiling – and therefore the amount of minerals that the water can carry is greater. The hot water rots the rocks at depth and carries away the dissolved elements, until somewhere along the route the temperature falls to a point where the mineral dissolves out of the water and fills up a vein or fissure with crystals. Different minerals tend to form at different locations as the water rises to the surface.

Such "natural refineries," powered by heat from the volcano, and operating over thousands of years, can create immense

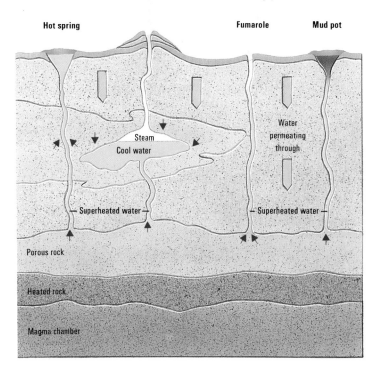

Ground water heated by magmatic intrusions re-emerges as hot springs, geysers or fumaroles.

Water heated by buried magma reaches the surface in the form of geysers, regular eruptions of steam, as seen (above left) at Yellowstone Park, Wyoming, Geothermal sources of energy may have practical as well as spectacular applications. In New Zealand (above right), geothermal energy is used to drive turbines for generating electricity.

mineral deposits. Other minerals, like sulfur or mercury, may be deposited directly from the gases emerging out of fumaroles.

Volcanoes can occasionally bring to the Earth's surface materials which would never be found naturally. Diamond is composed of the element carbon, and forms under very high pressures at depths greater than 60 miles in the Earth's mantle. Diamonds must be relatively common at that depth. Under exceptional circumstances, great outbursts of gas from deep in the mantle blast through to the Earth's surface, carrying a few of the diamonds with them. All our natural diamonds come from such old volcanoes, located in the continental interiors.

Harnessing the Earth's energy

The magmas from the mantle carry an additional resource – heat. Humans are always in search of heat to power industry and transport, and for domestic purposes. Almost all this heat comes secondhand, generally from the sun that shone millions of years ago on swamps, forests and shallow seas. This supported living organisms that died and passed into the rocks from which we now take their remains in the form of coal, oil and natural gas. Yet at depths of a few tens of miles, rocks are hot enough to melt. If only we could have access to the mantle, we would have an almost infinite supply of high-grade heat – there would never be an energy crisis again.

In most parts of the world, that heat is tantalizingly out of the reach of deep boreholes. But volcanoes achieve what the deepest borehole cannot hope to do: they bring the temperatures found at

The Geysers steam field in northern California uses pressurized steam from below ground to turn an electrical generator. Water from the steam is used to cool the generating equipment, and is then pumped back into the ground. Geothermal sources of energy such as these are in theory virtually inexhaustible, but since active volcanoes are seldom far away, the industry is not without its risks.

New energy from ancient rocks. At Penryn, Cornwall, deep boreholes probe ''hot rocks'', intrusions of magma from long extinct volcanoes. These may eventually be used to provide a cheap, safe and long-enduring source of energy.

depths of 30 miles up to the surface. Steam, formed when ground-water is heated by the buried magma, pours out at the surface as geysers, and has been used in Italy since 1904 to spin electricity-generating turbines at the Larderello Field. Today, similar geyser fields in California, Italy, New Zealand and Iceland have also been tapped to generate electricity.

However, natural geyser fields are not very common, and they also share a problem: what if the volcano associated with them should erupt? Already, in Iceland, a small eruption sent a column of red-hot magma shooting out of a geothermal borehole.

There are now attempts at Los Alamos, New Mexico and in Cornwall, England to use the heat of old hardened magma intrusions, from volcanoes long dead. The rock at depth has to be cracked to create paths for water that is pumped down from the surface and then heated to steam. The geothermal power plant is cheap to run, the process is harmless and long-lasting. The development of such techniques offers the possibility of using geothermal energy in countries, like Britain, where the last volcano erupted 50 million years ago.

The living planet Earth, shrouded in atmosphere, with a surface continually recreated by volcanic activity and colliding continents, contrasts with the unchanging, barren, meteorite-blasted lunar landscape.

We live on an unstable planet with a hot molten interior. For centuries, people believed they lived on a stable planet suffering only from the wrath of the gods. But we now know that earthquakes and volcanoes happen simply because we live on a planet whose interior is moving. Earth's outer shell is subject to great vibrations, when the brittle fabric of the exterior cracks, and red-hot gas and molten rock break through from within.

There are, nevertheless, certain benefits in living on an unstable planet. Without movements of the crust, new mountain ranges would not be created and the sea would have eroded all the land away; without volcanoes, we would not have our great wealth of minerals, already enriched in a way that would not occur on an old stable planet such as the Moon. Yet such arguments are not convincing – we had no choice in our planet home – and like any dwelling place, it has its advantages and its problems. When you stand on the crater's lip or experience the surging power of a great earthquake, it is difficult not to feel in awe of a mighty force that we can never hope to tame – yet as we understand its causes, we may hope to experience it with less dread.

Major earthquakes

There are many records of earthquakes in ancient writings, although these are almost always too fragmentary to be reconstructed. From around AD1200, enough information is available to define the larger earthquakes in regions where records were kept, such as Europe, the Middle East and China. However, only in the past century has it been possible to have a complete list of major earthquakes from around the globe. Even today an earthquake which kills 50 people in Pakistan or Peru may gain little publicity in Europe or America, while an event with a similar number of casualties in the West will be front page news. Therefore the list that follows cannot hope to be complete but simply covers some of the larger and most famous events.

| 1556 | Shansi Province |
| Jan 23 | China |

The earthquake which occurred in 1556 in the Shansi province of China was the worst natural disaster in recorded history. Tremors were felt in 212 of China's counties and widespread devastation occurred in 98 of those. There was an immense loss of life. The earthquake had struck at night, and many houses had collapsed onto their sleeping occupants. Additionally, many thousands of peasants who lived in hollowed-out caves within the unstable soft-silt (loess) cliffs perished when the massive earth structures crumbled.
Magnitude: 8.0/8.3
Death toll: 830,000 (est.)

| 1580 | England/Belgium/ |
| April 6 | France |

The largest earthquake in England in the past few centuries had an epicenter close to the Dover Straits. Damage to castles and churches was widespread through Kent, north France and Flanders. There are no records of the total casualties but at least two people died from falling masonry in London, 100 miles (160km) from the epicenter.

| 1692 | Port Royal |
| June 7 | Jamaica |

The tremors from this earthquake caused large-scale subsidence in the coastal town of Port Royal, built on an unstable foundation of gravel and sand. The majority of the town's buildings glided slowly into the sea, and lay relatively undisturbed for 250 years until marine archaeologists began systematic excavation.
Death toll: 2,000

| 1693 | Sicily |
| Jan 11 | Catania |

Two giant earthquakes have occurred along the seaboard of Eastern Sicily in the past 1,000 years. The huge 1693 earthquake destroyed 45 towns and cities including Catania, and caused thousands of deaths.
Death toll: 60,000 (est.)

| 1737 | Calcutta |
| Oct 11 | India |

Details of this catastrophe are lacking, due to inadequate historical records – but given

the reported number of victims, destruction must have occurred on a massive scale.
Death toll: 300,000 (est.)

1755   Lisbon
Nov 1   Portugal

Most of Lisbon's population of 250,000 were at church for All Saints' Day when the first shock struck at 9.40am on Nov 1. It was followed by an even more powerful tremor which sent buildings toppling down on the terrified populace. Huge waves crashed over the quays, drowning thousands and causing widespread damage. Fire rampaged through the ruins of the city for 3 days. The same earthquake and associated tsunamis also caused much destruction and loss of life further afield – approximately 10,000 died in Morocco.
Magnitude: 8.6
Death toll: 60,000

1783   Calabria
Feb 5   Italy

Between Feb 5 and Mar 28 1783, six major earthquakes shook the Calabria region of Italy. Massive destruction in 181 towns and villages resulted and many people died. The effects of the quakes were well documented – the first ever earthquake commission was set up, and produced a valuable detailed report: a real landmark in the history of earthquake science.
Death toll: 35,000

1811/   New Madrid,
1812   Missouri, USA

The earthquakes which struck North America in 1811-12 caused major landscape upheaval, though very few casualties due to the sparse population of the affected region. The main shocks occurred on Dec 16 1811, Jan 23 1812, and Feb 7 1812, and were felt most intensely in southeastern Missouri and Arkansas – although tremors reached as far as Washington DC and Pittsburgh, Pennsylvania. Massive fissures opened in the ground, forests were flattened, river courses were changed – a new lake appeared, and for a time the Mississippi flowed to the north.

Redfoot Lake, formed as a result of massive earth movements in the quakes of 1811-12.

The town of New Madrid was badly damaged, and subsequently destroyed by river erosions.
Magnitude: 7.5/7.3/7.8

1819   Rann of Kutch
June 16 India

Extremely violent over a very large area, with several

thousand casualties, this earthquake was felt up to 1,000 miles away. It is remarkable for the large area of land which sank underwater, and for the raising of a very long band (the Allah Bund – now understood as a fault scarp) traceable for many miles, and with a relative movement of up to 20ft.

1835	Concepción
Feb 20	Chile

A massive earthquake involving much ground displacement and coastal uplift. The destruction and subsequent tsunami were witnessed and investigated by Charles Darwin.
Magnitude: 8.5

1857	Naples
Dec 16	Italy

The widespread damage associated with this major earthquake was largely due to the inadequacy of local building techniques – 2 villages were completely destroyed, 2 more were partially damaged, and thousands were killed. The disaster was investigated very thoroughly by Robert Mallet, a pioneer in the new field of seismology. Mallet made meticulous records of all damage caused, and was thus able to calculate the approximate location and depth of the earthquake's focus.
Magnitude: 6.5
Death toll: 12,000

1872	Owens Valley,
Mar 26	California, USA

The Owens Valley earthquake

of 1872 was of major intensity and its shock waves travelled across most of Western America. Around the epicenter of the quake, landscape changes were drastic, with gaping fissures and sunken ground. The town of Lone Pine was all but obliterated, though the death toll was relatively light as a result of the buildings' largely wooden construction and the low population of the region.
Magnitude: 8.5
Death toll: 60

1886	Charleston,
Aug 31	South Carolina, USA

This rogue intraplate earthquake caused considerable damage in the city of Charleston and in the surrounding countryside, where railway lines were buckled, and great sand boils developed. The earthquake was felt over the whole of the eastern US.

1891	Mino and Owari
Oct 28	Japan

The provinces of Mino and Owari were both severely afflicted in the devastating earthquake which hit Japan in October 1891. The total disturbed area amounted to 330,000 sq miles (850,000 sq km), and within an area of 4,176 miles (6,700km) around the epicenter, 130,000 houses were destroyed, resulting in over 7,000 deaths. The earthquake was associated with extensive surface movement along a 70-mile (110km) fault line which ran through the island of Honshu.
Magnitude: 7.9

1896   Sanriku coast
June 15   Japan

The tsunamis generated by this tremor reached heights of up to 115ft (35m), and inflicted terrible destruction upon the town of Kamaisi and neighboring villages. 6,000 houses were swept away along with most of their inhabitants. Changes in sea level were recorded up to 5,000 miles (8,000km) away.
Magnitude: 7.5
Death toll: 27,000

1897   Assam
June 12   India

This major earthquake was one of the first to be studied from distant seismographs. A rapid undulating motion of the Earth's surface caused the destruction of all stone buildings within a 30,000 sq mile (78,000 sq km) area.
Magnitude: 8.7
Death toll: 1,500

1899   Yakutat Bay,
Sept 10   Alaska, USA

In terms of loss of life and damage to property, this earthquake was insignificant as it occurred in a very sparsely populated region – yet it was a major crustal movement. The area which was actually disturbed by the shock totaled about 300,000 sq miles (775,000 sq km). Avalanches crashed down mountainsides, and the coast line was uplifted by as much as 40ft (12m).
Magnitude: 8.5

1906   San Francisco
April 18 USA

Much of the city of San Francisco lay in ruins after this earthquake, which resulted from crustal movement along 270 miles (430km) of the San Andreas fault. Most of the

Haemorrhaging water mains left San Francisco powerless against fire.

damage was in fact caused by a post-quake fire which swept through the city.
Magnitude: 8.3
Death toll: 700

1906 Valparaiso
Aug 16 Chile

This high magnitude earthquake caused considerable coastal uplift and land deformation.
Magnitude: 8.6
Death toll: 1,500

1908 Messina
Dec 28 Sicily

Earth vibrations lasting a full 35 seconds devastated Messina in December 1908. Other towns and villages were also flattened, and a tsunami raged along the coast. There was marked evidence of major crustal movement – the coast line at Reggio, for example, was lowered by about 3ft.
Magnitude: 7.5
Death toll: 58,000

1920 Kansu Province
Dec 16 China

The great devastation caused by this notorious earthquake was due largely to poor soil conditions throughout Kansu province – intense shockwaves caused violent undulations of the thick loess, and several landslips resulted. An area 280 miles by 95 miles (450km by 150km) was severely affected by landscape deformation. 10 cities suffered widespread destruction and heavy casualties. The region had been earthquake-free for 280 years.
Magnitude: 8.6
Death toll: 200,000

1923 Tokyo
Sept 1 Japan

The earthquake which hit Yokohama and Tokyo in 1923 was one of the worst disasters of its kind in Japan. The ground shook for five long minutes as the Sagami Bay Fault ruptured. Thousands of buildings crashed to the ground, and a tsunami measuring 36ft (11m) burst against the coast. Most destructive of all were the fires that broke out – a mighty fire storm swept through Tokyo, burning people alive and destroying two thirds of the city's remaining buildings. A commemoration service is held in Tokyo on each anniversary of the catastrophic event.
Magnitude: 8.3
Death toll: 100,000

1933 Sanriku coast
Mar 3 Japan

The second occasion on which this coastal region of Japan fell victim to giant sea waves generated by a huge submarine earthquake. The tsunamis this time reached heights of 75ft (23m), destroying 9,000 homes and taking many lives.
Magnitude: 8.9
Death toll: 3,000

1960 Agadir
Feb 29 Morocco

The small quake which struck Morocco in 1960 occurred directly under Agadir, reducing the town to ruins within seconds. Thousands of bodies lay buried beneath the vast piles of rubble. In view of such utter destruction, reconstruction was considered

out of the question, and the area was abandoned.
Magnitude: 5.7
Death toll: 12,000

1963   Skopje
July 26   Yugoslavia

This shock struck Skopje at night – and most of the victims died in their beds as buildings collapsed on top of them. Property damage was immense, with the destruction of 16,000 houses.
Magnitude: 6.0
Death toll: 1,000

1964   Prince William Sound,
Mar   Alaska, USA

The so-called Good Friday earthquake which caused extensive damage in Anchorage, and generated several massive landslides. The resultant tsunami assaulted the Alaskan coast, and even claimed victims as far south as Crescent City, California.
Magnitude: 8.4
Death toll: 131

1968   Khorasan
Aug 31   Iran

The epicenter of the earthquake which hit Iran in 1968 was situated 8 miles (12km) beneath the Earth's surface, near the small town of Firdous. The tremor caused widespread destruction, taking many lives and leaving 60,000 people homeless.
Magnitude: 7.3
Death toll: 12,000

1970   Chimbote
May 31   Peru

The huge death toll which

resulted from this earthquake was mainly due to a resulting landslide, triggered at Mount Huascaran. A huge mass of rock and ice – some 80 million cu ft (2,000,000 cu m) in volume – hurtled down the slopes at speeds of up to 100mph (160kph), devastating everything in its path. The village of Yungay was completely overwhelmed with debris – most of the villagers and their dwellings were crushed beneath 30ft (9m) of mud and boulders.
Magitude: 7.8
Death toll: 67,000

1971   San Fernando Valley,
Feb 9   California, USA

This shock caused an estimated $500 million worth of damage to property. Mercifully, only 64 people died, due largely to the general good performance of the wood-framed houses.
Magnitude: 6.6

1972   Managua
Dec 23   Nicaragua

The effects of this earthquake were severe in an area of about 10 sq miles (25 sq km). In the city of Managua, 250,000 people were made homeless. Loss of life was high and more than 20,000 were injured.
Magnitude: 6.2
Death toll: 5,000

1975   Haicheng
Feb 4   China

This potentially destructive high magnitude earthquake was accurately predicted by the Chinese Seismological Bureau, and appropriate

advance preparations were made. A mass evacuation, involving about 3,000,000 people, was staged in which everyone was moved to fields and parks, away from the danger of falling buildings. When the earthquake struck at 7.36pm on Feb 4, property damage was extensive – the city of Haicheng lost 90% of its buildings – but casualties were miraculously light. This was a major success for the Chinese earthquake-watch program.
Magnitude: 7.3
Death toll: 1,300

1976 Feb 4   Guatemala

The Guatemala earthquake of 1976 was felt over an area of 40,000 sq miles (100,000 sq km), for the Motagua fault had ruptured along 150 miles (240km) of its length, causing poorly constructed dwellings to collapse onto their inhabitants. Thousands died, 77,000 were injured, and over one million were made homeless. Property losses were estimated to be in excess of $1 billion.
Magnitude: 7.5
Death toll: 23,000

1976 July 28   Tangshan China

This earthquake struck a densely populated area without warning, and thus its effects were devastating. Violent earth movements catapulted people over 6ft (2m) into the air. Serious damage occurred in Peking, 100 miles (160km) from the epicenter. Directly above the focus, 20 sq miles (50 sq km) of the city of Tangshan was flattened. Four

intense aftershocks caused further damage, and added many more to the casualty list.
Magnitude: 7.8
Death toll: 250,000

1977 Mar 4   Vrancea Romania

This earthquake was felt as far away as Moscow, though its epicenter was located under the Carpathian Mountains. Much destruction occurred in Bucharest – several apartment blocks were either destroyed or damaged and many people died.
Magnitude: 7.2
Death toll: 1,600

1980 Oct 10   El Asnam Algeria

The largest earthquake this century in Africa occurred in northern Algeria in 1980. It destroyed the city of El Asnam, rebuilt after a severe earthquake in 1954. Thousands died in the city and

Lessons for architects after the destructive earthquake at El Asnam in 1980.

surrounding towns and villages.
Magnitude: 7.2
Death toll: 3,500

1980   Campania
Nov 23   Italy

The earthquake which caused great damage in the old hill villages above the city of Naples was the most destructive in this region since 1857. Landslides contributed to the damage and blocked some of the winding mountain roads leading to the villages, hindering the rescue operation.
Magnitude: 6.9
Death toll: 3,000

1983   Coalinga,
May   California, USA

A moderate size earthquake originating from a hidden reverse fault. Damage was considerable but there were no fatalities.
Magnitude: 6.3

Main street, Coalinga, wrecked in the 1983 shock.

1985   Mexico City
Sept 19 Mexico

The large subduction zone earthquake beneath the coastal Michoacan region of Mexico caused extraordinary damage in Mexico City, 250 miles (400km) away. Regions in between were relatively unscathed. The damage was attributed to a very long period of shaking combined with amplification effects associated with the thick silt deposits from an old lake bed beneath the city center. About 1,000 buildings were destroyed, and over 10,000 people killed.
Magnitude: 8.1

1986   San Salvador
Oct   El Salvador

Although of relatively low intensity, this destructive earthquake hit the busy city of San Salvador in daylight hours, and hence casualties were heavy. Another seismic gap in this earthquake-torn region had been filled.
Magnitude: 5.2/5.4
Death toll: 400 (est.)

Major volcanic eruptions

Massive volcanic eruptions can be dated more easily than earthquakes, even when they have occurred before records were kept or in remote regions. The first three volcanic eruptions in the list that follows are ones known from detailed geological reconstruction – no eye-witness records survive. Most volcanic eruptions do little damage and some volcanoes, such as Stromboli north of Sicily, are permanently erupting. Thus the following list is only some of the most famous or deadly eruptions of the past centuries.

4,000BC (approx)	Mt Mazama Oregon, USA

A towering peak once stood where the famous Crater Lake is now situated, within a vast caldera in the Cascade mountains. This was the scene of a massive eruption around 4,000BC. From geological evidence, scientists have estimated that the explosion produced 5 cu miles (20 cu km) of airborne debris, and would have covered large areas of the northwestern United States with a blanket of ash. Viscous lava streams and glowing clouds from this monumental explosion inundated a large area. A gaping caldera 6 miles (10km) wide and 2,000ft (600m) deep was all that was left of Mount Mazama.

1450BC (approx)	Santorini Aegean Sea, Greece

Volcanic material found on the floor of the eastern Mediterranean provides evidence of a massive explosion that must have taken place around 1450BC. It is estimated that this eruption produced five times as much ejecta as Krakatoa in 1883; that the sound must have traveled as far as Scandinavia; and that sunlight was blocked out over the Mediterranean for several days. What is certain is that the explosion obliterated 32 sq miles (80 sq km) of the island of Thera, so creating a vast caldera. A fragmented crescent of small separate islands is all that is visible above sea level today. We have no clear records of other effects of this momentous eruption – however, some attribute the end of the Minoan civilization to it (though this has been recently disputed) and associations have even been made between Santorini and the mystery of Atlantis.

AD79 Aug 24	Vesuvius Naples, Italy

Aug 24 AD79 was the fateful day on which the cities of Pompeii and Herculaneum were to be blotted out by a sudden blast of furious activity from the long dormant Vesuvius. Rivers of hot mud, clouds of choking gases, and showers of ash and pumice descended on the two townships, completely burying all buildings and taking 20,000 lives. The two cities remained relatively undisturbed for 1600 years, hidden under 15–25ft (4–7m) of volcanic debris, until they were finally rediscovered and excavation began. Due to their remarkable state of preservation, the sites are of

Vesuvius threatens the bay and city of Naples

immense archaeological interest.

AD150   Taupo New Zealand

Lake Taupo, New Zealand, is a huge caldera, formed in a giant eruption in the past, when 14 cu miles (60 cu km) of debris was erupted, leaving a lake of 240 sq miles (620 sq km). Around AD150, in a series of eight enormous outbursts (the largest known eruption of the past two millennia), heavy ashfall blanketed almost all the North Island – 9,650 sq miles (25,000 sq km) receiving more than 4ins (10cm). In between the separate eruptions, vegetation had no chance to recover.

1538   Monte Nuovo Campi Flegrei, Italy

The formation of the volcanic cone of Monte Nuovo from the depths of an old crater lake in 1538 was the most recent outburst from the so-called Campi Flegrei (Phlegraean Fields). This is a region of persistent volcanic activity which apparently lies within a colossal crater, formed some 34,000 years ago. Recent dramatic ground movements of several feet under the town of Pozzuoli, situated within the Campi Flegrei, indicate another major upwelling of magma, and consequently suggest a new spate of volcanic activity in the not too distant future.

1669 March 11   Mt Etna Sicily

Europe's largest volcano, Etna has been active for thousands of years. In its eruption of 1669, massive ash clouds spread out over 60 miles (100km), and lava flow again threatened the long-suffering

town of Catania (inundated by the volcano's outpouring in AD122 and 1169). Although an old city wall held back the lava initially, the relentless flow eventually surged through to overwhelm several thousand people and their homes.
Death toll: 20,000

The ever-active crater of Mt Etna.

1759 Jorullo
Sept 29 Mexico

A volcano that was literally "born" in the eruption of 1759. The ejection of a dense steam cloud followed loud explosions – ash and cinders spread over a wide area, destroying the nearby village of La Huacan. The new volcano grew to mountain height over the next few years.

1772 Papandayan
Java

The explosive eruption of Papandayan in 1772 caused the whole northeast side of the volcano to collapse, generating massive landslides and hot mud flows. 40 villages were completely wiped out. The

catastrophe had reduced the height of the mountain from 9,000ft (2,700m) to 5,000ft (1,500m).
Death toll: 3,000

1783 Asamayama
Japan

Violently active since AD685, the 1783 eruption of this volcano was particularly explosive. Huge rocks were thrown in all directions – one was reported to have been 264ft (80m) by 120ft (35m). Large nuées ardentes were formed, along with catastrophic mud flows which buried 48 villages. This century, an observatory was set up nearby to monitor the volcano's behavior, so that future eruptions can be forecast and disaster avoided.
Death toll: 1,300

1783 Mt Laki
June 8 Iceland

This mighty eruption from a 19-mile (30km) long fissure poured huge quantities of basaltic lava over Iceland's landscape. Within 8 months, it had flooded a total area of 218 sq miles (560 sq km). There were serious economic consequences – the strong sulphuric fumes poisoned the island's crops, and half the livestock perished. One fifth of Iceland's 49,000 inhabitants died in the resultant famine.
Death toll: 10,000

1792 Unzen-Dake
Japan

An outburst of activity at Unzen-Dake in 1792 triggered a fatal landslide in which

18,000 cu ft (500 cu m) of mud and rock crashed down onto local habitations.
Death toll: 10,000

1815 Tambora Sumbawa, Indonesia

The sound of this massive eruption carried over 1,000 miles (1,600km), and ash was deposited over an area of 1,000,000 sq miles (2,500,000 sq km). One third of the volcano's total height was obliterated when an estimated 40 cu miles (160 cu km) of material was blasted into the atmosphere. The huge quantities of airborne debris appeared to have a severe effect on weather conditions – abnormally cold summers were reported worldwide. 10,000 people on Sumbawa and surrounding islands died as a direct result of the explosion. So too did thousands of wild and domestic animals, and the ensuing famine claimed another 82,000 lives.

1822 Galunggung Java

Galunggung has erupted only three times in history. In 1822, it exploded through its crater lake, generating a massive lahar 40 million cu yards (30 million cu m) in volume. All the countryside southeast of the volcano to a distance of 15 miles (24km) was coated with mud and 114 villages were destroyed.
Death toll: 4,000

1835 Coseguina Jan 20 Nicaragua

This was one of the biggest eruptions ever recorded. The huge ash cloud plunged an area of 50 miles (80km) radius into complete darkness. Airborne debris traveled as far as San Salvador 110 miles (180km) northeast, and the main explosion was heard in Kingston, Jamaica. The volcano had literally blown its top, violently ejecting an estimated 12 cu miles (50 cu km) of material, and leaving a gaping caldera 1.5 miles (2.4km) in diameter. There were no casualties.

1877 Cotopaxi June 26 Ecuador

Several of Cotopaxi's explosive eruptions have caused destruction and loss of life; that of 1877 was yet another in its violent history. The damage was largely caused by snow melting and triggering dangerous mud flows which devastated the surrounding countryside.
Death toll: 1,000

1883 Krakatoa Aug 27 Java

The eruption of Krakatoa in 1883 was one of the worst volcanic disasters in history. Dormant for 200 years, the 1,500ft (450m) high volcanic cone violently obliterated itself in a series of huge explosions heard up to 3,000 miles (5,000km) away. 5 cu miles (20 cu km) of rock and debris were blasted 15 miles (24km) into the atmosphere. Some smaller particles of ash reached to a height of 50 miles (80km), and proceeded to orbit the Earth during the following 2 years, causing spectacular red

sunsets worldwide. The subsequent collapse of the mountain top into the void beneath triggered tsunamis of gigantic proportions – one reputedly 100ft (30m) high. These huge waves (nine in all) raced towards the coasts of nearby Java and Sumatra and dealt one destructive blow after another, devastating 300 towns and villages.
Death toll: 36,000

| 1888 | **Bandai-San Japan** |

The fierce eruption of this volcano in 1888 produced a huge avalanche of earth and rock which buried 4 villages and partly destroyed 7 others. The total area of devastation was 27 sq miles (70 sq km).
Death toll: 500

| 1897 June | **Mayon Phillipines** |

Of the 26 eruptions of Mayon in the nineteenth century, the most destructive occurred in June 1897. Large quantities of ash were blasted into the atmosphere, and fell to earth as far as 100 miles (160km) away. Streams of lava flowed down over an area of 7 miles (11km) to the east of the volcano. Several hundred people died, and the town of Cagsuna was completely destroyed.

| 1902 May 7 | **La Soufrière St. Vincent** |

The eruption of La Soufrière in 1902 was preceded by small earth tremors. The climactic explosion of May 7 blasted a massive steam cloud up 30,000ft (9km), and sent a murderous nuée ardente rolling down the mountainside. Trees were flattened and scorched, houses were devastated, and hundreds died, mainly through inhalation of the hot dust. Great quantities of ash were deposited over a wide area.
Death toll: 1,500

| 1902 May 8 | **Mt Pelée Martinique** |

The catastrophic eruption of Mount Pelée in 1902 spelt doom for the town of St. Pierre and its inhabitants. Despite obvious warning signs from the volcano, orders for evacuation were not issued due to various intrigues concerning a forthcoming election. With characteristic precognition, various wild creatures staged their own mass evacuation – one area of St. Pierre was subjected to a nightmarish invasion of snakes. Then came the explosion itself, with the formation of a massive nuée ardente which bore mercilessly down on the town. Of a population of 30,000 people, only 2 survived, and every home was completely devastated.

In the last phase of its eruptive activity, the volcano produced lava which was too stiff to flow – hence the so-called "Tower of Pelée" was formed, growing at an incredible average rate of 30ft (9m) per day. It reached a height of 1,020ft (310m) before toppling to the ground.
Death toll: 30,000

| 1907 | **Bogoslof Aleutians** |

Bogoslof is a submarine

volcano in the northern Pacific which has emerged as a new island several times, only to disappear again beneath the waves. It broke the surface after a violent eruption in 1907, though its existence was soon cut short by the sea.

| 1911 | **Taal**
Phillipines |

The 1911 eruption of this volcano was a severe outburst. There was no lava flow, but ash was deposited over an area of 800 sq miles (2,000 sq km), and a killer nuée ardente was formed. The suffocating cloud claimed over one thousand victims.
Death toll: 1,335

| 1912 | **Katmai**
Alaska |

The eruption of Katmai in 1912 reduced a 7,500ft (2,300m) high peak to a gaping caldera 3 miles (5km) across. Three huge explosions were heard up to 750 miles (1,200km) away. Massive pumice and ash flows completely covered a nearby valley to a depth of over 800ft (250m), creating the so-called "Valley of Ten Thousand Smokes" which retained its heat for many years. Huge ash clouds cloaked the surrounding area in complete darkness for 60 hours, and ash fall spread as far as Kodiak, 100 miles (160km) away.

| 1914 | **Sakurajima**
Japan |

The volcano of Sakurajima exploded in 1914 after a series of mild earthquakes. The 20,000 natives had mercifully been evacuated to the city of Kagoshima, and were able to witness safely the volcano's spectacular display. A huge cloud rising to 30,000ft (9km) preceded the ejection of massive amounts of lava, which flowed down to fill the gap between the island and the mainland, so creating a peninsula. When people

Uneasy cohabitation at Sakurajima.

returned to the island, they discovered that 7 of the 18 villages had been destroyed.

However, an associated earthquake near Kagoshima at the time of the eruption struck a more tragic note. In the ensuing landslides, 35 people were killed and 112 injured.

1919	**Kelut**
	Java, Indonesia

The eruption of Kelut through its crater lake in 1919 generated a catastrophic mud flow. 104 villages were completely buried, and over 5,000 people lost their lives. An estimated 50 sq miles (80 sq km) of farmland was ruined. After the event, a tunnel was driven into the crater of the volcano, and the water level of the crater lake subsequently lowered, so that repetition of the disaster could be avoided. This safety measure was partially successful, although another disastrous eruption in 1966 wrecked the drainage system and caused further loss of life. A new tunnel has since been constructed at a lower level, secure from the effects of further volcanic activity.
Death toll: 5,110

1924	**Kilauea**
May	**Hawaii**

Kilauea on Hawaii is one of the world's most active volcanoes. Its many effusive explosions are not usually very dangerous – hence it can be studied at close range by volcanologists. In May 1924, a whole series of explosions sent ash clouds 4 miles (6km) up into the air, and huge rocks were blasted in all directions.

1931	**Mt Merapi**
	Java, Indonesia

Mount Merapi has erupted over 60 times since AD1006. In 1931, a large explosion produced a heavy rain of ash, together with a stream of lava 4 miles (6km) long, 200 yards (180m) wide, and 80ft (24m) high. Much loss of life and destruction resulted.
Death toll: 1,300

1835	**Mauna Loa**
Nov 21	**Hawaii**

Mauna Loa is the largest volcanic structure in the world, towering over 36,000ft (10,000m) above the ocean floor (13,700ft/4,000m) above sea level). It erupts frequently, producing copious quantities of highly mobile lava. Generally, these eruptions cause only minor damage – but lava flows do sometimes pose a threat to the nearby port of Hilo. On one such occasion – in November 1935 – lava streaming ominously towards the town was bombed by the United States Air Corps in an attempt to check its course. . The operation was successful, although sceptics argue that this was simply because the eruption had ceased.

1943	**Paricutín**
Feb 20	**Mexico**

The volcano of Paricutín was "born" on Feb 20 1943, with loud explosions that were heard over 200 miles (320km) away. It then proceeded to grow at an incredible speed, throwing out huge quantities of material (an estimated 3.6 billion tons in total). Within one year, the cone had risen to 1,000ft (300m). The residents of nearby San Juan Parangaricutiro were safely evacuated, and scientists took full advantage of the excellent opportunity to study a new volcanic outlet.

1951 Mt Lamington
Jan 21 Papua New Guinea

The long deafening roar of this major eruption was heard as far as 200 miles (320km) from its source. Huge ash clouds rose to a height of 40,000ft (12,000m) in 2 minutes, and a large nuée ardente, one of the most frightening of volcanic phenomena, was formed, This red-hot, dust-laden cloud devastated an area of 90 sq miles (230 sq km).
Death toll: 3,000

1952 Myozin
Sept Western Pacific

Explosions from a submarine source 250 miles (400km) south of Tokyo were first reported in September 1952. The new island which subsequently emerged was named Myozin, though it was soon to lose its battle for existence against the sea and disappear. Whilst trying to locate the resubmerged volcano, an unfortunate survey vessel (the *Kaiyo-maru*) with 31 men on board sailed directly over the very object of its search – precisely as Myozin began another spate of eruptive fury. All were killed.

1956 Bezymianny
Mar 30 Kamchatka, USSR

This major eruption of 1956

sent 1 cu mile (4 cu km) of debris surging up into the atmosphere in a giant ash cloud which reached 5 miles (8km) in height. A total area of 200 sq miles (500 sq km) was showered with hot ash, and melting snow soon created torrential mud flows. Fortunately there was no loss of life – in fact, people were able to safely witness this spectacular display.

1963 Surtsey
Nov 15 Iceland

The volcanic cone of Surtsey, off the coast of Iceland, first emerged above sea level in November 1963. Eruptive activity continued for a further 3 years, thus ensuring the island's survival against erosion by the sea (though this may ultimately be short-term).

1968 Mt Arenal
Costa Rica

This long dormant volcano burst into sudden activity in 1968. The strong explosion, in which huge blocks were catapulted as far as 3 miles (5km), was followed by the formation of nuées ardentes. 80 people were killed, and enormous damage to property resulted.
Death toll: 80

1973 Helgafell
Jan 23 Heimay, Iceland

The volcano Helgafell burst into new activity on Jan 23 1973 with eruptions through a mile-long fissure that opened on its flank. The 5,000 inhabitants of nearby Vestmannaeyjar were quickly

War between man and volcano on Heimay.

evacuated as the new volcano started to blast lava "bombs" towards the town, smashing windows and spreading fire. The new volcanic cone grew to 700ft (210m)in 2 weeks. The lava flow was sprayed with sea water in an effort to cool it down and thus check its advance towards the town and its harbor. The operation was largely successful, although Vestmannaeyjar still lost one third of its buildings. An estimated 1.3 million cu yards of lava had to be cleared away.

1976	La Soufrière Guadeloupe

74,000 people were evacuated from Guadeloupe when La Soufrière showed signs of activity. This large-scale operation was expensive and eventually proved to be unnecessary, as there was no major eruption.

1977 Jan 10	Nyiragongo Zaire, Africa

The lava lake at the crater of Nyiragongo had been seething with molten lava for several decades before the whole mountain split open along a fissure. At the lower ends of the fissure, 6,000ft (1,800m) below the crater lake, the magma poured out with such velocity that it overwhelmed several villages, killing more than 1,000 people. By 1982, the lava lake had refilled again.
Death toll: 1,200

1980 Mt St Helens
May 18 USA

Dormant for over 100 years, Mt St Helens roared back into life on May 18 1980 with incredible violence. A sudden earth tremor from within the mountain caused the entire north face to collapse, triggering an enormous landslide of rock and ice. Clouds of hot gas, ash and lava were blasted both laterally and vertically, reaching heights of up to 12 miles (20km). The eruption transformed 230 sq miles (600 sq km) of beautiful landscape into a gray wasteland of flattened scorched trees and thick mud and ash. Of the 60 lives that were lost in the disaster, most were simply taken unawares by the violence and scale of the eruption.

However, Mt St Helens did provide an excellent opportunity for volcanologists to study a volcano in action – detailed documentation of the cataclysm has been of immense value for volcano science.
Death toll: 60

1982 Galunggung
Indonesia

75,000 people had to be evacuated when Galunggung volcano began erupting on April 4 1982. In 1822, an eruption at the volcano had killed 4,000 people, but in this series of outbursts of ash, continuing through to August, only a few people lost their lives. Many villages all but disappeared under ash drifts; volcanic mudslides (lahars) followed when the rains came; and two 747 airliners en route to Australia were almost

brought down by sucking ash into their engines.

1982 El Chichón
Mar 28 Mexico

This eruption consisted of 3 major explosions over a period of 7 days, during which 500 million tons of ash was blasted into the atmosphere. The devastation was widespread, and several lives were lost, although the exact number is not known.

1985 Nevado del Ruiz
Nov Colombia

When Nevado del Ruiz volcano erupted in November 1985, torrents of water from melting ice poured down its flanks, forming massive mud flows which inundated the surrounding river valleys. An evacuation order was issued – too late, though, for the town of Armero, situated directly in the path of one of the lahars. As the great tide surged through the town, many of its buildings were buried in up to 12ft (4m) of mud, and most of the inhabitants were killed.
Death toll: 23,000

1986 Cameroon
Aug West Africa

This eruption consisted solely of a vast release of gas from a volcanic crater lake – there was no lava flow at all, yet still the consequences of the event were disastrous. The cloud of deadly gas – primarily carbon dioxide – rolled over a 6 sq mile (15 sq km) area around Lake Nios, overwhelming all those living in the vicinity. At least 1,500 villagers died of asphyxiation.

Glossary

Accelerograph An instrument that is triggered by vibrations. It can record, to very high resolution, the complete pattern of ground movements that comprise an earthquake.

Andesite The magma produced by a volcano located above a subduction zone cools to form a fine-grained gray rock known as andesite, richer in aluminum, sodium and calcium than a basalt.

Basalt The most common liquid rock (magma) erupted from a volcano or fissure which cools to form a fine-grained dark gray basalt. Basalts are mixtures of oxides, principally of silicon, magnesium, iron, calcium and aluminum.

Benioff zone The band of earthquake centers dipping away from the oceans and reaching depths of 400 miles (700km). It defines the subduction zone, where oceanic plate returns down into the mantle.

Caldera A deep, round, generally water-filled lake or marine basin, formed from the collapse of a volcano into its own magma chamber after a major eruption has expelled all the magma.

Crater The hollowed-out summit area of a volcano which may be filled with rubble or may connect directly with the hollow volcanic vent which brings fresh eruptions to the surface.

Crust The outermost shell of the Earth composed of lighter "granite" rocks richer in silica than the underlying denser mantle. Between 12 and 43 miles (20–70km) thick beneath the continents but only 3 miles (5km) thick beneath the oceans.

Epicenter The point at the surface immediately above the location of a sudden fault movement that generates an earthquake.

Fault A planar zone of weakness passing through the rocks of the crust, along which movement of one side relative to the other has taken place.

Fumarole A hole in the side or summit of a volcano from which gas and steam issue.

Geothermal Heat obtained from the enormous energy reserves of the Earth's hot interior.

Geyser A natural hot water and steam fountain created by steam pressure produced through contact of underground streams with hot buried volcanic rocks.

Hotspot A rising column of hot rock from deep in the mantle melts to form magma which burns a path through the plate, producing surface volcanoes. As the plates are moving relative to the Earth's interior, the hotspot volcanoes appear to gradually shift with time although it is actually the plate that is moving.

Ignimbrite When red-hot magma filled with gas is erupted very rapidly and in very large quantities, the particles do not have time to solidify before they fall back to the Earth's surface. Enormous heaps of part-molten magma fragments become welded together into a tough rock known as ignimbrite.

Intrusion When a large mass of magma solidifies underground, it forms an intrusion. Intrusions may have many shapes – from huge fat domes (laccoliths) to narrow sheets which are known as dykes when they are near vertical, and sills when they lie parallel with the geological layers.

Island-arc A garland of islands arranged in an arc with a deep ocean trench located on the seaward side. The individual islands are andesite volcanoes lying above a subduction zone.

Lahar A volcanic mudslide often formed during an eruption when hot ash mixes with water from melting ice and snow, a pre-existing crater lake, or heavy rains.

Lava Molten rock or magma that has flowed to the surface from the mouth of a crater or fissure. Lava can mean the molten, part-molten or solidified magma.

Liquefaction When the grains within a water-saturated soil become more tightly packed, as with an increase of pressure or prolonged vibration, the material may take on the properties of a quicksand, sometimes flowing out at the ground surface. This is known as liquefaction.

Magma Liquid rock.

Mantle The large majority of the Earth, from beneath the crust to depths of 1,800 miles (3,000km), composed of dense silicates of magnesium, iron, calcium and aluminum.

Mercalli Scale of Intensity A measure of the severity of earthquake vibration at a particular surface location on a 12-point scale devised by the Italian seismologist Guiseppe Mercalli.

Moho (Mohorovicić discontinuity) The boundary between the mantle and the crust.

Moment A measure of the energy of an earthquake calculated from the area of the fault that moved multiplied by the displacement and the rock rigidity.

Nuée ardente A glowing cloud of gas and magma fragments, erupted in a sudden outburst, that rolls down the side of a volcano as a red-hot avalanche.

Phreatic An eruption caused by the "flashing" of water to steam with an enormous increase in volume.

Plate tectonics The theory of the outer shell of the Earth based on the pattern of global earthquakes. Regions generally without earthquakes are the rigid plates, about 60 miles (100km) thick, that move over the softer mantle. Narrow corridors of earthquakes define the plate boundaries where the plates move relative to one another.

Plinian   The term defining the distinctive eruptive cloud which forms a towering column of ash and smoke in the shape of a pine tree. It was first observed and described by Pliny the Elder in the AD79 eruption of Mt Vesuvius.

P waves   The first vibrations (P for Prima) to arrive from a sudden fault movement are compressional waves that travel through the ground like sound waves in air.

Radon   A radioactive inert gas produced by the decay of natural uranium in rocks. Because it is formed amidst the rocks, a sudden build-up of radon at the surface may indicate that the rocks are being rapidly squeezed, as can occur prior to a large earthquake.

Resonance   Vibration in harmony. An object will be in resonance if its natural period of vibration (or in musical terms, its pitch – like the pitch of a tuning fork) is the same as that of some external vibration or sound.

Richter scale   A scale for determining the size of an earthquake from the trace of the vibration registered on a seismographic instrument. The maximum amplitude of the vibration is adjusted for the distance of the earthquake center from the instrument. Named after the Californian seismologist Charles Richter, who invented it.

Seiches   Regular disturbances of water level, produced in lakes and rivers, by the passage of very long period seismic waves, often at great distances from a very large earthquake.

Seismic gap   That part of a major active fault zone identified as not having moved for the longest time period, and therefore most prone to moving next.

Seismograph   An instrument that continuously records and amplifies ground vibrations on a magnetic tape or smoked paper drum.

Shear (S) waves   Vibrations that pass through the rocks with a side-to-side motion, traveling slower than the initial P (Prima) waves. Shear waves cannot travel through liquids.

Spreading ridge   A plate boundary at which new ocean crust is created by the eruption and intrusion of basaltic magma arriving from the mantle.

Subduction zone   The zone down which the oceanic plate passes into the mantle.

Tsunami   Japanese for "wave in the harbor," and used to define a water wave that is generated by a sudden change in the sea bed from an earthquake fault, landslide or volcanic collapse. Tsunamis, unlike wind-waves, involve the whole body of water to the sea bottom. They travel at speeds of up to 300mph (500kph) in the open ocean, slowing and banking up into enormous waves (as high as 90ft/30m) in the shallow waters close to land.

Index

Acknowledgments

T = top   B = bottom   C = center   L = left   R = right
Cover: Soames Summerhays/Science Photo Library. Title Page: Armstrong/ZEFA. Aldus Archive 13T, 64, 66–67, 70–71, 94, 120 (Tad Nichols); Bryan & Cherry Alexander 36; Tempest Anderson/The Yorkshire Museum 129; Anglo-Chinese Educational Institute 20 (Liu Dongao), 80–81 (Guan Tianyi); Ardea 10, 46B (Francois Gohier); Art Directors Photo Library 43BL (Craig Aurness), 43BR, 87, 88, 89, 91C (Chuck O'Rear); Loftus Brown 50; California Historical Society, San Francisco 139B; Bruce Coleman 79 (James Simon), 98–99 (Werner Stoy), 100T (G D Plage), 103 (Melinda Berge), 127B (Keith Gunnar), 133 (Nicholas Devore); Daily Telegraph Colour Library 5 (Chris Bonington), 112, 113 (Krafft), 115 (L L T Rhodes); E T Archive 107; Frank Lane Picture Agency 16–17, 71, 96 (Steve McCutcheon), 95, 101 (S Jonasson), 101B; Gamma/Frank Spooner 51 (Naythons), 56, 74; Geoscience Features Picture Library 102, 110, 126–7 (University Film Service), 127T; Susan Griggs 73; Leslie Herbert-Gustar/Patrick A Nott 26; Michael Holford Library 76–77 (Gerry Clyde); Italian State Tourist Office (E.N.I.T.) London 145; Japan National Tourist Office 149B; The Mansell Collection 12–13; Robert Muir Wood 41, 48, 49T, 49C, 76, 118R, 137, 142B, 146; NASA/Science Photo Library 82, 135; New Zealand Herald 124–5; Nigel Press Associates 108–9; Planet Earth Pictures 109 (Krov Menuhin), 116 (Flip Schulke), 132L (Jane Camenzind), 132R (Robert Jureit); Popperfoto 9, 14, 27B, 43T, 63B, 65, 67B, 68C, 85; Principia Mechanica Ltd 72; Science Museum, London 27C; Sipa/Rex Features 16, 19, 63C (Manoocher), 90–91, 91T (Frilet), 122–3 (El Tiempo); South American Pictures 6–7, 22 (Tony Morrison); Spectrum Colour Library 55B; Eileen Tweedy 30T (Royal Society), 40 (SOAS Library); US Geological Survey 46T, 52–53 (J K Hillers), 143B; Anita Wagner 77; J Watton/Camborne School of Mines Geothermal Project 134; Woodmansterne 39 (Anthony Britton), 101T, 118L (John Guest); ZEFA 37, 68T (W Janoud), 69, 111 (Falconer), 117 (Damm), 152T.